MOVING FORWARD
with LITERATURE CIRCLES

How to Plan, Manage, and
Evaluate Literature Circles That
Deepen Understanding and Foster
a Love of Reading

Jeni Pollack Day

Dixie Lee Spiegel

Janet McLellan

Valerie B. Brown

SCHOLASTIC

PROFESSIONAL BOOKS

New York • Toronto • London • Auckland • Sydney • Mexico City
New Delhi • Hong Kong • Buenos Aires

This book is lovingly dedicated to
Grace and Norm Pollack–JPD
Freddie–DLS
My family–JM
My family and friends–VBB

Cover design by Vito Zarkovic
Interior design by Holly Grundon
Cover and interior photographs by Peter Hvizdak

ISBN 0-439-17668-9
Copyright © 2002 by Jeni Pollack Day, Dixie Lee Spiegel, Janet McLellan, and Valerie B. Brown
All rights reserved
Printed in the U.S.A.

Contents

◆ **CHAPTER 1** ◆

Situating and Setting Up Literature Circles 12

◆ **CHAPTER 2** ◆

Preparing Students for Literature Circles 30

◆ **CHAPTER 3** ◆

Encouraging Real Discussion 54

◆ **CHAPTER 4** ◆

Writing and Thinking in Response to Literature Circles 84

List of Strategy Lessons

List of Rubrics for Assessing Literature Circles

Acknowledgments

We are deeply indebted to all those who helped make this book a reality. Thank you to the wonderful people at Scholastic, particularly Wendy Murray, who provided this opportunity as well as substantial encouragement and fantastic editorial advice, and Ray Coutu, editor, cheerleader, and writing instructor, who responded to our writing as we hope to respond to our students, with clarity, insight, and infinite kindness.

This book could not have been written without the support of amazing teachers, administrators, and other colleagues with whom we have worked. These people have shaped our thinking about teaching and helped us feel we have something worthwhile to say. Thank you for your comments, your questions, and your honest skepticism that make us continue to rethink issues and question our choices.

We are grateful for Jeni's wonderful students at the Forest View School in Durham, North Carolina, who participated in our data collection, and considered themselves honored to do so, giving their opinions thoughtfully and honestly. We are also thankful to the other teachers and students with whom we've worked on literature circles, in particular, Mary Sances and her fifth graders at the Condon School in Boston, who appear in many of the photographs in the book.

Finally, to the people closest to us who provided invaluable support:

- Jeni would like to thank her parents, Norm and Grace Pollack, and parents-in-law, Billie and Joe Day, who provided both space to write and continual enthusiasm for the book; Maggi and Elaine, the best girlfriends a girl could have; Jo for the house at the lake and many long walks; and Laura, who provided Jeni a place in which to write and fortified her with ice cream, pasta, and all things chocolate. And, most of all, thanks to Gregory Day, who knew she could do this long before she had a clue.

- Dixie would like to say thanks to Mary Zolman who got her interested in literature circles in the first place.

- Janet would like to thank her family, Paul and Nicholas Brichta.

- Valerie is grateful to her family who supported her efforts in writing this book. She appreciates their patience as she spent many hours at the keyboard, working until the wee hours of the morning. She would also like to thank her close friends who encouraged her every step of the way.

About the Authors

 **JENI POLLACK DAY** is a doctoral candidate in reading education at the State University of New York, Albany, and a research assistant at the Center on English Learning and Achievement (CELA). She also teaches fourth grade in the Boston Public Schools, at the Fuller School in Jamaica Plain, Massachusetts.

 **DIXIE LEE SPIEGEL** is a professor of Literacy Studies at the University of North Carolina, Chapel Hill, where she teaches graduate and undergraduate courses. She is a former third-grade teacher and Title I reading teacher. Her articles have appeared in many journals including *The Reading Teacher, Language Arts*, and the *Journal of Reading Behavior*.

 **JANET McLELLAN** is an assistant professor at the University of Hawaii in the Division of Speech Pathology and Audiology, where she teaches graduate and undergraduate courses. She has worked extensively in the public schools as a speech-language pathologist and as a special education teacher.

 **VALERIE B. BROWN** is the Vice President for Programs at the Wake Education Partnership in North Carolina, an independent advocacy group supporting public schools, and a monthly columnist for *Scholastic News*. She has had extensive experience as a classroom teacher, reading specialist, Reading Recovery teacher, and professional development coordinator.

Foreword

*I*t is actually quite remarkable that so many of us have managed to ignore the importance of developing students' capacity for engaging in conversations around literature. For some reason we have focused much more attention on developing their proficiency for answering questions—usually so-called comprehension questions that require only a one-word or single-sentence response. Perhaps it is the influence of standardized testing that has driven such practice. Or maybe it is just a powerful aspect of the "grammar of schooling" that Tyack and Cuban (1995) so powerfully analyze. They note that almost all American adults, including teachers and administrators, experienced "school" in the traditional sense and, therefore, expect certain features of "schooling" in today's curriculum. One of those features is that students will be asked lots of questions after they have read something. When post-reading questions disappear from school lessons—replaced by discussion, for instance—adults perceive it as a violation of the grammar of schooling.

Regardless of the reason, creating post-reading questions receives much more attention in teacher-education programs and reading-curriculum materials than fostering classroom discussion. Yet, a considerable body of evidence strongly indicates that discussion fosters improved understanding. For instance, Knapp (1995) found that when teachers in high-poverty schools offered lessons with opportunities for students to discuss what they had read, reading achievement improved. Fall, Webb, and Chudowsky (2000) reported that performance on reading comprehension tests rose dramatically when students had even brief opportunities to discuss the test passages with peers. Allington and Johnston (2001; 2002) noted that conversation was characteristic of the classrooms of more effective elementary teachers. And, finally, Guthrie and Alvermann (1999) report that increasing opportunities for classroom discussion enhances students' motivation to read. The point is that a research base supports shifting from classroom lessons that are less interrogational to ones that are more conversational.

Further, real-world evidence shows that few adults interrogate each other after reading. Instead, they discuss what they've read. They share their impressions, delve into the accuracy and believability of the text, compare themselves to characters, and so forth.

Moving Forward with Literature Circles provides a powerful and practical guide to changing classrooms so that students are able to engage in conversations around literature. It provides a close look at one remarkable classroom where students acquire the skills and strategies they need to talk about the texts they read with others—talk that enhances their understanding.

This book was created to answer the many and varied questions that arise as teachers attempt literature circles as a way to move away from interrogation into discussion.

- Who chooses the books to read?
- How do you ensure that kids engage in productive conversations?
- How do you evaluate comprehension through discussion?

The authors address those questions and others in a straightforward, thoughtful manner. They supply an array of instructional tools that any teacher might use to develop and support a purposeful classroom filled with engaging discussion of the characters, motives, design features, personal interpretations, and individual responses to texts of every sort. Of the many educational books published every year, there are only a few I wish I had written. *Moving Forward with Literature Circles* is one of them.

—*Richard L. Allington*

Fein Distinguished Professor of Education

University of Florida

References

Allington, R. L., & Johnston, P. 2001. "What Do We Know aAbout Effective Fourth-Grade Teachers and Their Classrooms?" C. Roller (ed.), *Learning to Teach Reading: Setting the Research Agenda.* Newark, DE: International Reading Association.

Allington, R. L., & Johnston, P. 2002. *Reading to Learn: Lessons from Exemplary Fourth-Grade Classrooms.* New York: Guilford.

Fall, R., Webb, N. M., & Chudowsky, N. 2000. "Group Discussion and Large-Scale Language Arts Assessment: Effects on Students' Comprehension." *American Educational Research Journal,* 37(4), 911-941.

Guthrie, J. T. & Alvermann, D. 1999. *Engaged Reading: Processes, Practices, and Policy Implications.* New York: Teachers College Press.

Knapp, M. S. 1995. *Teaching for Meaning in High-Poverty Classrooms.* New York: Teachers College Press.

Tyack, D., & Cuban, L. 1995. *Tinkering Toward Utopia: A Century of Public School Reform.* Cambridge, MA: Harvard University Press.

Introduction

About This Book

*I*n the summer of 1996, while finishing her master's degree at the University of North Carolina, Chapel Hill, Jeni Day found herself in a course on reading comprehension taught by Dixie Spiegel. The friendship that developed between Jeni and Dixie led to a year-long collaboration on literature circles in Jeni's fifth-grade classroom. Janet McLellan and Valerie Brown, then doctoral students at the university, quickly joined them to help with planning, problem solving, data collection, and the eternal tape transcribing. *Moving Forward With Literature Circles* is the result of those efforts. While work since 1996 is well represented here, the authors owe a great deal of their thinking about literature circles to their conversations and accomplishments of that year.

The book begins with a chapter on situating and setting up literature circles, which introduces how and why Jeni carried them out. To help you understand her decisions, we talk about the assumptions behind discussion groups as a powerful way of engaging children and deepening their responses to literature. Then we present the daily schedule we used for each literature discussion cycle.

In Chapter 2, we describe a five-stage plan for helping students develop the independence necessary for participating fully in literature circles. We share goals for each stage, strategy lessons for helping students become skilled at discussion, and samples of student discussions. Finally, we emphasize the importance of time in setting up literature circles that work.

Chapter 3 defines real discussion and shows how it differs from other forms of group talk. We explore more deeply the importance of discussion in response to literature. And we have a reality check in which we present our hopes for literature circles, the realities of what often happens, and strategies for moving toward the ideal.

The purpose of Chapter 4 is to look at writing in literature circles from several different perspectives. First we describe how writing enhances discussion of

literature. Next we describe one kind of writing we used with our groups—
journals—and give examples of the kinds of writing and thinking that took place.
We then talk about responding to writing. Finally, we review several ways to
help children think more deeply about text through writing.

In Chapter 5 we explore the purposes and content of assessment. We describe
what to assess (such as what children talk about), how students interact in their
groups, and how they think about literature, along with ideas on how to gather
information and interpret it.

As part of our research for this book, we followed four diverse learners in
Jeni's class. In Chapter 6, we make the case that literature discussion is especially
critical for diverse learners. We describe these students, how they participated
in literature circles, and what we learned from them. Then we describe interventions to help non-traditional learners succeed in literature circles.

Moving Forward With Literature Circles is designed for classroom teachers,
reading teachers, and school administrators from third grade through middle
school. We hope you find it useful and that it gives you the courage to try
literature circles in your own classroom.

CHAPTER 1

Situating
and Setting Up
Literature Circles

E very Tuesday, Jeni's fifth-grade students meet in literature circles. Jeni begins each meeting with announcements, reminders, and, usually, a strategy lesson. The children then take their books and response journals to various corners of the room and huddle in groups of three to five, on the floor, at desks, and under tables, to discuss the chapters of the novel or the short story they have all read and written about during the previous week. While discussions often begin with a prompt to get the group thinking, the students usually move onto other topics and ideas quickly and spontaneously.

A literature circle is an opportunity for a small group of children to talk together about a text. This is not unstructured talk time, but, rather, focused discussion on characters and events, personal experiences that relate to the text, and observations of the writer's craft. As children share their opinions and reflect on their

reading experiences, their comprehension grows in sophisticated ways. Unlike traditional discussions, in which the teacher poses questions to get the students to think in a particular way, literature circles provide a context for children to ask their own questions and help each other answer them. As Schlick Noe and Johnson note, "Collaboration is at the heart of this approach. Students reshape and add onto their understandings as they construct meaning with other readers" (Schlick Noe and Johnson, 1999).

To help you understand Jeni's decisions, we explore the assumptions behind discussion groups as a powerful way of engaging children and deepening their responses to literature. We also present the daily schedule used for each literature discussion cycle.

"I don't know if I can give you a specific example, but like somebody says something, and then another person can say, 'Well maybe think about it this way, or think about it another way.'"

—*Kelly*

A Real Discussion

Rather than try to describe a literature circle discussion, let us share one with you. This discussion among three students occurred early in the school year, after the class had listened to Jeni read *Baseball Saved Us* (Mochizuki, Lee & Low). This story is about a Japanese-American boy in an internment camp during World War II, for whom baseball becomes a way to deal with his family's incarceration.

Drew: I think that the book was okay. But, I mean, if he couldn't hit a ball, that's not that good. I don't think he would have hit a home run all of a sudden.

Tanya: I don't know. You can tell where this book is made up at because if he can't hit a ball, how can he make a home run? This doesn't make any sense.

Lucy: I think that I kind of liked the book, but I think it would have been even more interesting, if it was like a girl, that she was still Japanese, and she like could hit a ball because then she could get to first base and stuff. But it wasn't a very catchy book. It was kind of yucky.

Drew: At the end, I don't know if that really might have happened, because he saw [the glare on his sunglasses], a baseball player wouldn't wear sunglasses. They do, but they usually wouldn't. A pitcher wouldn't because it would give him a glare in his eyes.

Lucy: How come whenever he hit a home run he was looking at somebody with sunglasses on? I mean that's a little strange because when he sees a glint on the sunglasses, he hit a home run.

Tanya: I don't see how baseball saved him. I don't see how baseball saved him.

Lucy: Yeah, I know. The title has nothing to do with the book except like baseball . . . Or I guess they mean like baseball . . . they did have to live there without doing anything and just sitting around and everyone getting mad at everybody else.

Tanya: I don't think he really knows how to play baseball. He can't hit a home run.

Lucy: Actually, the book said he could. They said that he could usually hit base hits, but he thought he was no good because he usually struck out. It's like, um, he had a fifty-fifty chance that he's going to hit a base hit or strike out, and then all of a sudden he got real mad, and he just got real mad and he hit it, so in a sense he had so much force that it just went out, so that's why I think he hit it.

Drew: I don't think he could have hit it with everybody booing because that would have really gotten in your mind.

While this discussion may seem rudimentary, a closer look reveals remarkable sophistication in some of the responses:

◆ **The students show that they understand characters and plot.** Rather than answering simple factual questions (*Who were the main characters? Why did they do what they did?*), these fifth graders evaluate the characters' actions ("*I don't think he could hit it with everyone booing.*") and consider alternative characters as possibilities ("*The main character ought to have been a girl.*"). They also understand the sequence of plot events as proven when they address the boy's final burst of anger that helps him hit a home run.

◆ **The students articulate confusion and look for sense in the book.** ("*I don't see how baseball saved him.*" "*How could he suddenly hit a home run when he can't even get a base hit?*") They use evidence from the text to make a case for their opinions, such as when Lucy says, "*Actually the book said he could.*"

◆ **The students use their own experiences to elaborate on what the text is about**, for example when Drew talks about trying to play with people booing or whether baseball players wear sunglasses. Wondering about the appropriateness of the title helps them begin to hypothesize about the theme of the book. They also discuss the book's primary theme, for example, when Lucy wonders if baseball gave them something to do to prevent them from becoming edgy and impatient with one another.

◆ **The students make inferences based on the text.** Lucy says, "I guess they mean . . . " and then suggests how the title might fit the story. Tanya remarks, "I don't think he knows how to play baseball. He can't hit a home run."

◆ **The students see themselves as competent to evaluate the book.** Drew says it is "Okay, but . . . " Lucy comments that the story is "yucky" and then gives reasons for her opinion. They critically examine what is in print, pointing out where the realism of the story breaks down (*"You can tell where the story is made up . . . "*) and use their own experiences as evidence. For example, Drew and Tanya both mention the likelihood of hitting a home run when the main character couldn't even get a base hit. Finally, Lucy theorizes that his anger made it possible for him to hit a home run, and she remarks that being bored might make your family impatient with one another. Here, Lucy uses evidence from the story and her life to elaborate the other group members' observations (For more on assessing discussion, see Chapter 5.)

The fifth graders in this example did all of these things in less than three minutes of discussion, without direct supervision. While Jeni prepared them, the students arrived at discussion points on their own.

From this experience we realize that students are competent to discuss and teach one another. Because Jeni lets go of control, and gives them an opportunity to make sense of the story through discussion, we are able to see what students are capable of doing themselves. We also become more aware of each student's growth and progress in reading.

Abilities Students Demonstrate During Literature Circles

◆ Articulate confusion and formulate questions

◆ Identify and use information about literary elements such as characters, plot, and setting

◆ Identify and use information about literary techniques such as metaphor, symbolism, and foreshadowing

◆ Use strategies to maintain comprehension and increase engagement, such as inferring, predicting, questioning, theorizing, and evaluating

◆ Interpret the text by using evidence from the text

◆ Interpret the text by applying their own experiences

◆ Find the central meaning or theme of the text, as well as alternative or sub-themes

◆ Evaluate the text based on their own experiences and imagination

---

Other discussions show not only that students are capable of knowing definitions of literary terms and devices (such as character, theme, plot, and setting) and of strategies (such as predicting, inferring, and asking questions), but also that they can use them in making sense of books. Furthermore, we learn that when students work as a group, they can understand the book far better than they can alone.

The Benefits
of Literature Circles

W e began our work with literature circles by focusing on five important benefits of using them with students.

LITERATURE CIRCLES HELP YOU TO TEACH—NOT MERELY CHECK— COMPREHENSION

Reading comprehension is often misunderstood in teaching. While we talk about teaching comprehension, what we often do is not actually teach it, but merely measure it (Wendler, Samuels, and Moore, 1989). When we give students something to read and ask them questions about it, we aren't teaching them to comprehend; we are checking to see if they *did* comprehend. When we "drill" them on their reading, we don't make the processes of understanding explicit. We don't provide the opportunity to "see" what comprehension looks like as we read.

In literature circles, we can see the processes of comprehension unfold. We can see comprehension deepen and expand as students share their experiences and questions with a group. This "window on comprehension" is one of the most powerful aspects of literature circles. Discussion helps strong readers gain more control over comprehension strategies by explaining ideas to their peers. It allows struggling readers to see comprehension modeled and practice it. That is precisely what was happening when a less proficient reader, Tanya, questioned the text by stating, "*I don't see how baseball saved them,*" and a much stronger reader, Lucy, modeled her process of thinking about what the title might mean.

Sometimes we teachers are more concerned with having students learn the name of a strategy than actually applying it. For example, Duffy (1993) observed teachers who taught students the definition of a compound word, but not how to use that knowledge to help them when they came to words they didn't know. While students could identify and define compound words, they did not get better at decoding them and continued to have problems with compound words in their reading. Knowing definitions for strategies is not the same as using the strategies.

If children believe that the purpose of reading is to understand and enjoy a text, and if they have the opportunity to read lots of interesting and reasonably easy material, they learn to read strategically with comprehension. Both children and adults remember, understand, relate, interpret, and evaluate based on their own experiences without necessarily being conscious that they are doing so (Smith, 1998). But, rather than build on what children do naturally, we teachers sometimes tend to come with our own agenda of strategies to teach. While these strategies are often very valuable, they are useless unless children have the opportunity to relate them to what they already know and can do, and to have lots of practice using them. Literature circles provide that practice.

LITERATURE CIRCLES ALLOW YOU TO TEACH MANY FACETS OF COMPREHENSION

What does it mean to say we understand or comprehend a story? Do we "comprehend" if we can identify the characters or put plot events in sequence? Do we understand the story if we can explain the symbolism or the theme the author is trying to get across? Do we have to relate to the characters or feel as if we understand ourselves or others a little better? Do we need to be able to relate the story to our own life to understand it? In the *Baseball Saved*

Facets of Comprehension

- ◆ Remembering character, plot, setting, theme

- ◆ Appreciating literary devices

- ◆ Noticing connections across texts, making inferences, predicting

- ◆ Making connections to our own lives

- ◆ Evaluating the text

Us discussion, for example, each fifth grader begins with a basic understanding of the story, the characters, and the storyline, but that is only the beginning of their comprehension.

There are many facets of reading comprehension. It is important to be aware of them so that we know exactly what we are trying to promote when we devote valuable time to literature circles. One facet is remembering characters, plot sequences, setting, and theme. For another facet we note symbolism and appreciate literary devices, such as metaphor and mood. Still another lets us notice connections across texts, make inferences, use foreshadowing, predict, and then check those predictions. Another allows us to make connections with our own lives, experiences, and knowledge. Another lets us critically evaluate text by imagining ourselves being or having a conversation with the author or seeing the text as a reflection of society and its values. Here we notice inconsistencies, wonder about the relevance or logic of events or character behavior, or determine the veracity of what we read (Day, 2000). Literature circles provide children the opportunity to go beyond learning superficial facts about a book, beyond guessing what "experts" think the book is about, to finding personal meaning.

LITERATURE CIRCLES ENCOURAGE STUDENTS TO LEARN FROM ONE ANOTHER

> "Literature circles are important because you get to hear what other people are feeling, you know, and what they think. And they're the ones that help you to change your mind, 'cause of what they say. It's fun to discuss books and see what everybody else feels."
>
> *—Lucy*

Would it surprise you to know that two of the three students in the *Baseball Saved Us* discussion were not even close to being the most fluent readers in the class? Drew was receiving special education services, and Tanya scored in the lowest quartile on her fourth-grade standardized reading test. Yet Drew used his knowledge of baseball to reflect on the authenticity of the story. Tanya modeled questioning by articulating what she didn't understand and what conflicted with her understanding. By asking questions she also helped the group discuss, rather than report on, the book. (For more on the difference between discussing and reporting, see Chapter 3.) Lucy, a much stronger reader, modeled for Tanya and Drew how to think about a title's meaning, the possibility of questioning the author's choices, and following up on other group members' ideas. Each of these children brought a different perspective to the story, and each contributed something unique to the group's understanding of it.

LITERATURE CIRCLES MOTIVATE STUDENTS NATURALLY

Literature circles are motivating to children for a deceptively simple reason: Talking about what you learn is fun. After starting literature circles, Jeni began to see students talking animatedly about what they were learning. She compared it with seeing a movie with friends:

"I rarely walk out of a movie theater silent. My friends and I—and almost everyone around us—leave talking about the movie. Mimicking the funny lines of dialogue, questioning inconsistencies, checking to see when each person figured out any mystery in the movie, piecing together plot twists and foreshadowing, inferring relationships and then checking them with the group. Later on, we share the parts we consider most important with those who haven't seen the movie, and recommend that they see it or not, based on our own evaluation."

> "I had a good time with my discussion group . . . I liked what we were talking about and we got really into it. We all had a lot of comments on everything."
>
> —Drew

Further, our own comprehension of the movie deepens through this conversation. We often have a stronger appreciation of, or objection to, a movie after discussing it. This is exactly what happens in a literature discussion. We give students an opportunity to share their thoughts, questions, and theories, and in the process, they think more deeply about the story.

LITERATURE CIRCLES PROMOTE DISCUSSION MORE EFFECTIVELY THAN WHOLE GROUPS

Whole-class discussions about literature are valuable. In fact, as you'll see in Chapter 2, Jeni began teaching the children about literature circles through whole-class discussions, and she ended each literature circles session with a whole-class debriefing about the discussions that took place. But small groups offer certain advantages that whole-class discussions don't.

Literature Circles Promote Discussion by:

♦ giving more opportunity for everyone to talk.

♦ providing a more natural context for conversation.

♦ encouraging responsibility and independence.

♦ making it easier to find text at an appropriate reading level.

♦ offering students more choice of what they read.

Small groups give more opportunity for everyone to talk.
For many students a small group provides more opportunity to talk for the simple reason that there are fewer voices. But a small group is also a less stressful environment in which to share. In a large group, only a few, generally the most confident and outgoing, are comfortable talking. Furthermore, in a small group students may be more likely to share tentative ideas that haven't been thought through completely. Tentative ideas are riskier to tell a group than carefully thought out opinions, but they are critical to literature discussion because they allow the group members to build an understanding, rather than convince each other of individually formed opinions.

Small groups provide a more natural context for conversation.
Whole-class discussions tend to be more formal and traditional. As adults, we rarely find ourselves in a discussion with more than a few people. The closest thing in real life might be a community gathering, such as a PTO meeting. But a PTO meeting is formal and governed by rules to promote order. With large-group discussion, there is far less opportunity to respond to individual ideas or to move the discussion in different directions that might meet the needs of the participants. The agenda, rather than the needs of individuals, governs the nature of the conversation. The same is often true for whole-class discussions. The teacher and the most vocal students carry the discussion.

Small groups encourage responsibility and independence.
When several groups are meeting simultaneously in a classroom with just one teacher, the students take over responsibility for the group, and make it their own. This independence is important. When we are learning something new, we often find it easier to let the expert perform the task so we avoid looking clumsy. So, too, when children are learning to hold a discussion, they often let the teacher take

control. For example, Jeni noticed that when she joined a group, discussion frequently stopped and the children looked to her for direction. Once she left, they felt more comfortable taking initiative and speaking independently.

Small groups make it easier to find text at an appropriate reading level.
When you are dealing with fewer students, it is easier to find something each student can read comfortably. Research has shown that students get better at reading when reading materials are at their independent level. They need to be engaged mostly with books they can read comfortably on their own (Allington, 2001, 1983). We also know from research that children who are less skilled readers and who are least motivated to read spend most of their school time reading books that are too difficult. (Allington, 2001, 1983; Berliner, 1981; Gambrell, Wilson, and Gantt, 1981; and Stallings, 1980). Can you imagine how most of us would feel about reading if books by Dickens, Tolstoy, and Hawthorne were the only ones available to us?

It is more enjoyable and, therefore, more motivating to read books you can read easily or comfortably. When preparing for a vacation, we rarely go to the library and choose the longest, hardest book on the most abstract topic we can find. We choose to read more difficult books sometimes, especially if we are particularly interested in the topic, but most often we like to read books that we find a pleasure to read. Small groups, in which each student has participated in the selection of the book, make this a far easier goal to reach.

> "I like the little group better than the whole class because there's not as many people that have to talk so you can talk more or let other people talk more . . . . I just like it better because each person has more time to talk and lots more time to listen and you can explain things better."
>
> *–Caryll*

Small groups offer students more choice of what they read.
As with reading level, small groups make it easier to come to consensus on books of interest. In a class of 28, finding a book that everyone wants to read is an impossible task. The solution is often based on teacher preference or majority rule, or more likely, based on what is available in multiple copies. While small groups don't eliminate this problem, they make negotiation easier ("I'll read your book if we read my book next"). An added bonus is that multiple copies of books are far

easier to find in sets of four or five, something we did by borrowing from other classrooms, the school's media center, and the public library.

Having choice is motivating. As adults, we get book recommendations all the time, but we read only books that appeal to us. If we had to read only what was suggested by another person, we would probably begin to dislike reading and dread the recommendations. While most of us like to have titles suggested to us, we also like to have the final say in what we read, and so do our students.

Structuring
Literature Circles

With these five benefits in mind, we developed a schedule for literature circles in Jeni's class. We generally did literature circles once a week, for one hour during Language Arts time. This was our plan, of course, which can be modified to fit your curriculum and the needs of your students. This schedule could easily be adapted to two or three days a week, or a daily program.

Why did we do literature circles only once a week if they were so valuable? First, literature circles were something new for the students and Jeni, and this schedule allowed everyone to learn the process gradually, without frustration and without taking time away from other activities. We had read professional books and articles on literature circles that advocated devoting the entire reading program to them and we wondered how teachers got there, and even if they should be there. It seemed like a pretty big step to make overnight. We preferred to take it slowly.

Second, there are many other important components to Jeni's literacy program, such as writers' workshop, independent reading, guided reading, read-aloud, word study, integrated social studies and science, and drama. She has to organize and balance her time carefully.

Third, beginning slowly is important for teachers who have unsupportive or cautious administrators. It's easier to get acceptance to take 60 minutes a week from a schedule for one new element than to completely overhaul the reading program.

Typical Schedule for a One-Hour Literature Circle Session

Student Preparation: Ongoing

During the preceding week, the students prepare for literature circles by reading agreed-upon chapters and writing a pre-discussion entry in their journals.

Teacher Directions, Announcements, and/or Strategy Lesson: 5–10 minutes

Jeni reminds students of strategies they've learned previously and presents a strategy lesson to enhance discussion of literature.

Small-Group Discussion: 15–25 minutes

The groups discuss what they have read using their journal entries as a guide. They negotiate chapters they will read for the next discussion and what prompt–or question–they will use to get ideas flowing.

Journal Writing: 5–10 minutes

Students write a post-discussion journal entry, telling how their ideas about the text have or have not changed.

Whole-Group Debriefing: 15–20 minutes

The whole class discusses what went on in their circles, what worked, what didn't, and why.

STUDENT PREPARATION: ONGOING

Students prepare for literature circle sessions by reading the agreed-upon chapters of a novel and writing a journal entry based on a prompt that the group has chosen. (See Chapter 4 for more on journals and page 98 for examples of prompts.) Groups use this journal entry as a starting point into their discussion. Early in the year, students do their preparatory reading and writing during an assigned time in class. As the year progresses, and they take over responsibility for their groups, reading their novel and writing in their journals becomes their homework.

TEACHER DIRECTIONS, ANNOUNCEMENTS, AND/OR STRATEGY LESSON: 5–10 MINUTES

The teacher reminds the class of discussion from a previous session ("Remember we've been talking about how to ask questions of group members if you don't understand or agree with them?") or any other helpful information ("Don't forget, I'm collecting groups x's and y's journals, and no groups in the back corner because of the science fair projects.") Strategy lessons are also conducted during this time on topics such as relating the text to personal experience, noticing character development, or reflecting on how discussion changed their ideas. (Ideas for strategy lessons are scattered throughout Chapters 2 through 5.) Following the lesson, students move into groups around room with their journals and books.

SMALL-GROUP DISCUSSION: 15–25 MINUTES

The groups meet to share their thoughts about the reading. They start by discussing journal entries, based on the prompt, and move on to discussing parts they like and dislike, parts they found confusing, and so forth. At the end of the discussion, the groups negotiate the chapters they will read for the next meeting and the prompt—the discussion-generating question—they will write about in their journals, for example, "Have your feelings about the main character changed?" During the small-group meetings, the teacher circulates and listens in on discussions, often from a distance if her presence might stifle or influence the discussion. The teacher may join a group if the students are having a difficult time, but her primary purpose is to listen. This is time for the students to talk. (For more on discussion, see Chapters 2 and 3.)

Appendix 5

Group Meeting Log – [Completed after each discussion by group together or individuals   Date ___4/12___

Group members present ___Caryll Lucy, Adele Kate___

Group members absent _____

Did everyone read the chapters and prepare a journal entry? (yes)

Book and Chapters read for today ___The Midwife Apprentice chpts___

Prompt(s) ___Are you like the main character?___

How did your group feel about this prompt?

(use it again)   don't like it   use it often

Topics discussed _____

We are nothing like the main character on the outside

Good things that happened today.

Everyone had something to say
Everyone listened and asked questions.

_____

Were their any problems today?

We didn't get the prompt at first but Mrs. Day helped.

How did your group go today? Was this better/worse than other groups in which you have participated?

this was a good group. we all had a lot of things to says.

After each meeting, groups fill out logs like this to help students reflect on their learning and prepare for whole-class debriefings.

Students write in their journals before meetings to prepare for the discussion, and after meetings to think through issues connected to the book and the group.

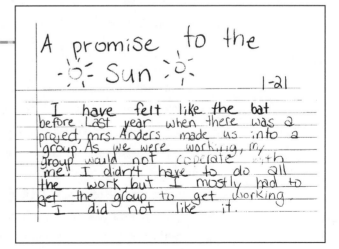

A promise to the Sun   1-21

I have felt like the bat before. Last year when there was a project, mrs. Anders made us into a group. As we were working, my group would not cooperate with me!! I didn't have to do all the work, but I mostly had to get the group to get working. I did not like it.

Journal Writing: 5–10 minutes

As the groups disperse, students return to their desks to write a second journal entry, explaining how their thoughts about the book have changed or stayed the same as a result of the discussion. The students may also write about any concerns they have regarding group dynamics. One member of each group reports to the teacher during this time on what their group read, what they discussed, and what their goals are for next time. This report is one way Jeni keeps track of each group's progress. (For more on writing and sample journal entries, see Chapter 4. For more on assessment, see Chapter 5.)

Whole-Group Debriefing: 15–20 minutes

The class meets to reflect on the nature of the discussion, good things that happened, topics that came up, and their concerns. The students and teacher reflect on the experience of that day, bring up problems, and share ideas for solving them collectively.

By doing this final stage as a whole group, students benefit from everyone's experience. When a problem is identified, such as forgetting what you wanted to say because the conversation went so quickly, other students can relate to and learn from the experience. Whole-group discussion provides awareness into the different problems, a particularly valuable asset. It also allows students to share good things that happened. Further, students can brainstorm solutions to problems. We have been amazed at the sophisticated solutions they are able to identify, as well as their willingness to implement their own solutions.

Beginning and ending with class reflection is one of the most valuable parts of literature circle sessions, and one of the things that keeps discussions fresh and interesting. From the beginning, we have encouraged students to reflect on their book and what their group talked about, but, even more, to reflect on the process of the discussion.

Discussing a book is a complex task requiring students to listen and respond to each other, go to the text for evidence, form hypotheses and predictions, and look for complex themes and answers. Along with that, students have to get along and work together and take responsibility for their reading and writing, in addition to the discussion. This is a lot to ask. It requires a different way of thinking about learning and school. Shifting thinking about something is possible, but it requires time, patience, and self-reflection.

Final Thoughts

We wrote this book to help you guide your students in thinking differently about learning and literature. Although we provide specific ideas for getting there, it is not a recipe book to be followed exactly, but, rather, a story to use as a foundation for teaching that meets the specific needs of your students, your school, and yourself. In the next chapter, you'll learn how we introduced the concept of literature circles and prepared students for them.

CHAPTER 2

Preparing
Students for
Literature
Circles

S usan is another fifth-grade teacher at Jeni's school. When she expressed an interest in trying literature circles early in the school year, Jeni was happy to share what she knew. Susan devoted a week to literature circles and then went back to Jeni with reason after reason for why they were a disaster. In her words, "The kids simply can't do it." She went on to say that the students either sat in silence or talked about sports or other topics unrelated to the book. When she wasn't there, the students didn't discuss the book. Susan was convinced that literature circles had no value and were a huge waste of valuable "teaching time."

Susan is a good teacher, but what we learned from her experience is that this is not a program that can simply be put into place and left alone. A great deal of

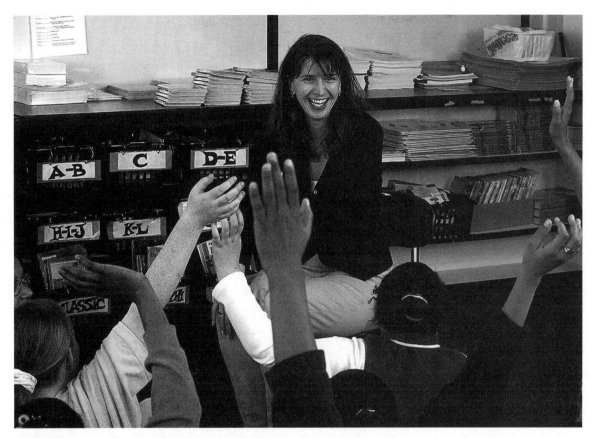

Before placing students into groups, Jeni spends time talking with them about the purposes, pitfalls, and values of literature circles.

time and effort need to be devoted to it if students are going to benefit from it. You need to plan on giving the program plenty of attention, moving students gradually toward independence at a pace that reflects a growing ability to discuss thoughtfully and work independently. You need to assume there will be problems from day one and that problem solving will need to be a part of your planning. Indeed, if problems are embraced as opportunities to improve, rather than seen as evidence of failure, the process of learning with your students will be one of the best parts of literature circles.

In this chapter we begin by sharing our five-stage plan to guide students toward working independently in literature circles. As part of the plan, we include strategy lessons that help students develop independence at each stage.

Our Five-Stage Plan
for Preparing Students

Before Jeni organized students into literature circles, she carried out a plan designed to build the skills necessary for substantive, independent discussions. She started by reading stories aloud and facilitating a whole-group meeting about them. She then conducted several lessons in which she read short selections aloud and had children discuss the selections in small groups, using a prompt she chose. Next, she selected a short story for students to read independently and discuss in small groups. Then, she placed students in groups and allowed them to choose books and prompts to spark the discussion. Finally, in addition to choosing their own books and prompts, students could choose their own groups.

Each of these stages is presented in detail in this chapter, along with strategy lessons to support each stage. We encourage you to modify the plan to suit your classroom. We carried it out over a period of 12 weeks; you may want to modify the time. Remember, flexibility is essential.

SETTING THE STAGE: INTRODUCING STUDENTS TO THE CONCEPT OF LITERATURE CIRCLES

Before beginning the plan, conduct one or two whole-group lessons to introduce literature circles and develop discussion guidelines. Start by saying something like this: "We are going to do something called literature circles every week. In literature circles, you discuss a book or story with a small group of classmates who have read the same book or story. Literature circles are fun and you will learn a lot. You'll find that you think a lot more about a story when you discuss it with others. Hopefully, you'll have opinions. Others in your group will have different opinions that will be interesting, too. They will also have questions about things they didn't understand, and perhaps you will also have questions. You can help one another answer them. So let's begin by thinking about what makes for a good discussion and develop some guidelines to help us in our groups."

Jeni works with the entire class to establish guidelines for good discussions.

Creating a list of discussion guidelines is a vital first step in setting up literature circles. By involving students in generating the list, you encourage them to think about what it takes to make a discussion work. Students also become more willing to follow the guidelines because they understand why they are in place and have had a stake in choosing them.

DEVELOPING DISCUSSION GUIDELINES

OBJECTIVE: To create and refine guidelines for good discussions, as a class

MATERIALS: Chart paper, slips of paper with behaviors for a mock discussion written on them. (See ideas on the next page.)

STEPS:

1. Have students talk to one another about their experiences with discussions they enjoyed and ones they did not. Based on those experiences, have them write down their definition of "a discussion" and what makes for a good one.

2. Discuss students' ideas in a whole-group meeting.

3. Choose ideas that students consider most important for a good discussion, and create a class list of guidelines on chart paper.

4. After developing the guidelines, have students model discussions, exaggerating both good and poor behaviors. Ask four students to choose from slips of paper with typical behaviors written on them. The students then have a mock discussion, acting out their behaviors, while the rest of class tries to guess what they are.

5. As the students act out different scenarios, stop them occasionally so the class can discuss what is happening, natural consequences of the actions, and strategies for changing the behaviors if necessary. For example, when a student engages in disruptive behavior, note that it is impossible to have a discussion that flows because of constant interruptions. Then have the students brainstorm ways to stop a classmate from being disruptive.

Guidelines Jeni's Class Developed

- Everyone listens; everyone talks.

- Come prepared by having read the selection and written in journals.

- Pay attention to everyone.

- Avoid side conversations.

- Use only kind comments, no insults.

- Disagree agreeably; tell why you don't agree.

- Ask questions if people don't talk.

- Change the topic after everyone has had a chance to talk.

6. Following mock discussions, look back at the guidelines you created and think about other difficulties that might arise, as well as other factors that make for successful discussions. Note students' observations on chart paper.

It's important to provide students with regular opportunities to "debrief" about the success of their literature circles. Allow them to discuss problems, suggest solutions, and modify the guidelines accordingly.

Possible Poor Behaviors to Act Out

◆ "Me First" interrupts, does not respond to what other people say, and ignores everyone else in the group. Instead of listening to others, "Me First" pipes up with her own thoughts and ideas that she expresses in an arrogant tone.

◆ "I'm Right" pouts when her ideas are challenged, is not open to others' opinions, and is insistent that her ideas are always right. She makes comments like, "I read the entire book and I know that you are wrong about everything and I am right!"

◆ "Rather Rude" calls people names, interrupts, talks too loudly, and ignores members of the group. She also looks at her fingernails instead of listening, speaks with an obnoxious voice, and calls her classmates names.

◆ "Space Cadet" rarely participates, is ill prepared, looks around the room, is out of her seat often, and usually is off-topic when she does participate. Her comments about the book are irrelevant to the conversation.

Carrying Out the Plan

STAGE ONE: ENGAGING STUDENTS IN WHOLE-GROUP DISCUSSIONS

GOAL: To model what to talk about in literature circles

(TWO TO FOUR LESSONS)

A key to successful literature discussions is helping students reflect on what they are doing. Unless they know what the process is about, they remain dependent on you to tell them what to say and how to solve problems. The goal for stage one, therefore, is to help them think about the process of discussing. What is okay to do and say in literature circles? This is important in helping students move quickly to having their own discussions.

In stage one, the teacher reads a short story or a picture book aloud to the class. After listening to a story, the students respond in their journals to a teacher-selected prompt such as "How did the story make you feel?" or "What parts made you feel this way?" The teacher then guides a discussion with the whole class. After the discussion, students respond in their journals again. Finally, the teacher holds a whole-class meeting to discuss the process.

Here is a transcript of a whole-group discussion Jeni conducted with her students, based on "Camp Fat," a short story from the book *Altogether, One at a Time* by E.L. Konigsburg (Aladdin Books). In this funny story, a girl's parents send her to a weight-loss camp. While she's there, she meets someone who encourages her to think about both inner and outer beauty.

Jeni: We are going to discuss this story I have just read. This is going to be different from "real" literature circles because I will be here and because we will all be sharing as a whole class. That means that everyone won't get to talk as much. I hope that you will still listen to each other and think about the book. So . . .

Good Read-Aloud Books for Stage One

Sleeping Ugly by J. Yolen (Coward-McCann)

The Wretched Stone by C. Van Allsburg (Houghton Mifflin)

Baseball Saved Us by K. Mochizuki (Lee & Low)

Working Cotton by S. A. Williams (Harcourt, Brace, Jovanovich)

Our Plan at a Glance

Stage/ Goal	Group Size	Text Used	Prompts	Time-Frame
1. To model what to talk about	Whole group	Short stories or picture books read aloud, teacher selected	Teacher selected Example: "How did the story make you feel?"	2–4 lessons
2. To give students practice discussing stories	Small groups, teacher organized	Short stories read aloud, teacher selected	Teacher selected Example: "Would you have done what the main character did?"	2–4 lessons
3. To have students discuss a story that they read on their own	Small groups, teacher organized	Short stories read by students independently, teacher selected	Teacher selected with student input Example: "With what event does the author really catch your attention?"	2–4 lessons
4. To move students toward selecting, reading, and discussing full-length texts	Small groups, teacher organized	Chapter books read by students independently, student selected	Student selected and generated	4–8 lessons
5. To have students choose books, organize groups, and conduct discussions independently	Small groups, student organized	Chapter books read by students independently, student selected	Student selected and generated	The rest of the year

does anyone have a thought about our prompt, which was, "Have you ever felt like the main character in the book?"

[*Jeni pauses and looks around trying to catch students' eyes.*]

Jeni: Maybe we should start out with what she was feeling. What was she feeling?

Kelly: She felt ugly and fat.

A.J.: She was angry because her parents made her go to fat camp and she didn't want to.

Ryan: The girl was not happy because she got no snacks.

Evan: She was mad.

A.J.: Yeah, like her parents just sending her off to camp, I mean, that's not fair.

Jenna: I think she was most mad because her parents, because they sent her to camp, her parents actually thought she was fat. It would hurt if your parents thought something like that about you.

Evan: Plus you're angry because you don't want to do it.

Kate: I think that if my parents did that to me I'd be really angry, because normally they ask me if I want to go somewhere but sometimes I have to go, and I don't like it.

Kelly: You know, you could tell for the main character, that that would be torture, she liked chocolate so much and you don't get to eat that much at fat camp.

Caryll: Yeah, you'd always be hungry.

[*Students continue to discuss what the character was feeling at the beginning of the book. To get them thinking about the rest of the book, Jeni shifts the direction slightly.*]

Jeni: Think about the blob Miss Natasha gave the main character. How many of you think you would have bothered with it?

Kate: I would have bothered because you knew there was something really important in there.

Jenna: I would probably bother out of curiosity, you know.

Tanya: I don't think I would have bothered with it, because it says it smelled really bad, I mean, I really hate to touch things that don't smell good.

[Students laugh.]

Drew: I might have started it, but then not finished it.

Jeni: Can anyone think of times your parents made you do something? I mean if you share your stories, it might help us think about how Clara felt about being sent away to fat camp.

Tanya: Sometimes my mom makes me play with my cousins. I really don't like them because they are mean.

Jeni: So what do you do? Are you like Clara or not?

Tanya: I usually play with them, but I don't like it, so I guess I'm not as bad as Clara.

Annie: My parents forced me to go to an overnight camp and I really didn't want to go.

Jeni: Were you terrible about it or good?

Annie: I was terrible, but I was really mad at my mom. I didn't talk to her for three days. I was so unhappy, and I know she was really unhappy, but I was so mad at her.

Evan: I think everyone's parents make them do things they don't want to do, but it's important how you deal with it.

Caryll: Sometimes it's worth doing, and sometimes it isn't worth doing . . . . I guess that's what Clara had to decide.

While this discussion is more about making personal observations and less about responding to one another, there are two important things happening. First, the students understand that using their stories and experiences to understand the book is part of literature circles. Second, they carry most of the conversation. Jeni asks questions, but she rarely shares her opinions.

It is often difficult for us teachers to remain silent and let children talk. We feel we aren't teaching if we aren't talking. Also, we like to talk, and teachers are used to being the most important voice. We need to change this if our students are to tap their own stories and experiences and stop depending upon us to do their thinking for them.

Tips for Getting Kids Talking in Whole Groups

Here are a few suggestions for getting students to speak up, especially if they are not used to it.

1. Be quiet! Students can't talk if you do.

2. Avoid evaluative comments such as, "that's good," "that's smart," "that's thinking," and so forth. Praise reinforces your role as teacher and makes children dependent on you. You want them to know they have made a good comment because it develops conversation, not because you said it was good. They can't develop sensitivity to that if you chime in with an evaluation.

3. If you must respond, show how their comment develops the conversation. Talk about what a student comment brought to mind. Provide a genuine response, something you would say to another adult in conversation. "I hadn't thought of that before . . . You know, that makes me think of . . . I'm not sure I agree, because in my experience . . . "

4. Model the type of comments you want students to make. Students will copy what you say, so say what you hope they will repeat.

5. Don't stare at the speaker when he or she is speaking to a classmate. Instead, look down or away. If students can see your eyes, they will wait for you to take the lead. But if you focus your attention elsewhere, they are more likely to take the lead. This helps the listeners, too. By looking down or away, you encourage them to look to the speaker, rather than to you, for feedback.

6. If no one talks, look around and try to catch children's eyes. Catching a person's eyes often nudges them to talk.

7. Sit opposite silent students, adjacent to talkative ones. Reticent children, like adults, are more likely to talk if they catch an encourging glance.

8. Learn to accept silence, but rephrase a question or statement if you need to. There is a fine line between too little and too much wait time. When students are silent for too long, it is probably because they don't know what to say. Consider rephrasing what you're asking them—for example, in the transcript above, when Jeni rephrases the question "Have you ever felt like the main character in the book?" to "What was she feeling?"

Strategy Lesson — REFLECTING ON WHOLE-GROUP DISCUSSIONS

OBJECTIVE: To help students recognize what is acceptable to say and do in literature circles and how they can think about the kinds of responses group members make

MATERIALS: Chart paper

STEPS:

1. After the first or second whole-class discussion of a story, ask students to think about what happened. Encourage them to "take apart" the experience. For example, say something like this: "Let's take a step back and pretend we are visitors observing this discussion and we are not sure what just happened here. Can anyone describe what we just did?"

2. Provide open-ended questions, or prompts, to spark their thinking, such as: What kinds of things did we say? What were you thinking about during the

What We Do in Literature Circles

- Share what makes sense

- Share what doesn't make sense

- Ask others' opinions

- Ask each other questions

- Share our stories that help us understand the characters in the book

- Share what we might do if we were the character

- Listen to each other

- Use others' ideas to help us think

discussion? Can you describe how your thinking changed from before the discussion to afterwards? If you had to try to describe what you learned here today, what would you say? What was your favorite part of today's discussion? When the discussion slows down, what types of things do you notice get it going again?

3. If students have a lot to say, break them into small groups to brainstorm lists and then bring them back to share. If students aren't sure what to say, keep them together as a whole group.

4. As a whole class, create a list on chart paper of what happened during the discussion. Entitle it, "What We Do in Literature Circles." See the sidebar for the list Jeni created with her group of fifth graders.

5. Post the chart so you and the students can add to it from time to time.

STAGE TWO: MOVING STUDENTS TO SMALL-GROUP DISCUSSIONS

GOAL: To give students practice discussing stories in small groups

(TWO TO FOUR LESSONS)

The objective here is to move students into small-group discussions gently, starting with a whole-class read-aloud. Because the teacher reads the same story to the entire class, all students have access to the text, making the subsequent discussions, and debriefing session, more meaningful.

For each lesson in stage two, the teacher selects a somewhat longer text, such as a short story, and reads it to the students. The students respond in their journals and then move into teacher-selected small groups to discuss the story. The teacher provides the prompts, as in stage one.

Focusing and sustaining discussion is one of the most important things students need to know when first moving to small groups. Good prompts can help them. Prompts are questions that target general aspects of a text or broad areas of thinking. Prompts have no "right" answers. Two prompts that Jeni's students used often were "Would you have done what the main character did?" and "Would you recommend this book to someone else? Why or why not?" Another popular prompt was "How are you like the main character in this book?" (For a complete list of prompts, see Chapter 4.)

Here is a strategy lesson that familiarizes students with prompts and helps them reflect on which prompts work best in various situations.

Strategy Lesson · FOCUSING THE DISCUSSION WITH PROMPTS

Because the teacher is often not present in a small group to get a discussion started or keep it focused, we have to teach students how to do this themselves. While other authors have recommended the use of roles or jobs (for example, see Daniels, 1994), we prefer stimulating the discussion through prompts. One risk of prompts is that they can limit the extent to which students explore a text. But if you help students reflect on the benefits and possibilities of different kinds of prompts, they become more adept at choosing ones that are best for particular circumstances—and more invested in the resulting discussions.

OBJECTIVE: To familiarize students with different kinds of prompts

MATERIALS: Photocopied list of prompts for each student (See page 98.)

Good Story Sources for Stage Two

Storyworks (Scholastic)

Cricket magazine

What Do Fish Have to Do With Anything? by Avi (Candlewick Press)

Altogether, One at a Time by E.L. Konigsburg (Aladdin Books)

The Big Book for Peace by A. Durell and M. Sachs, editors (Dutton)

The Big Book for Our Planet by J.C. George, A. Durell, and K. Paterson (Dutton)

Angels and Other Strangers by K. Paterson (HarperCollins)

STEPS:

1. Hand out photocopied lists of prompts and have students read through them silently.

2. In small groups, have students sort prompts into the following categories:

   - good for picture books versus chapter books
   - good for beginning a book versus ending one
   - harder to answer versus easier
   - make for an interesting discussion versus a less interesting one

3. Have students share discuss their observations with the whole class. Be sure to allow them to disagree and share their reasons.

4. Later, once they have used the prompts in a literature circle, have students report back during the whole-group debriefing whether their predictions were correct.

STAGE THREE: MOVING STUDENTS TO INDEPENDENT READING

GOAL: To have students discuss a story that they read on their own
(TWO TO FOUR LESSONS)

In stage three, students read short stories independently, rather than having stories read to them. The teacher selects the story and gives students ample time to read it on their own. Because they have experience with prompts, they brainstorm a list of possibilities from ones they know and have used successfully, and choose one to get the discussion going. After reading the story, they respond to the prompt in their journals, discuss in small groups, and debrief as a whole class.

Using Controversy to Start and Sustain Discussion

A good discussion is usually open ended, with participants bringing up and dismissing topics all the time. This free flow of ideas is usually difficult for students to grasp at first and needs to be scaffolded. Jeni finds that controversy works wonders, not only to spark discussion, but also to sustain it. Ongoing discussion often arises from students searching for a correct answer to a question that has no correct answer, such as, "With what event does the author really catch your attention?" or "Should this book have won an award?" Questions like these can spur rich discussions as students attempt to come to some sort of agreement. By forcing consensus where it shouldn't exist, you push each student to make a case for his or her opinion.

OBJECTIVE: To help students dig into a discussion and defend their points

MATERIALS: Short story for students to read

STEPS:

1. Provide students with a short story to read and time to read it.

2. Give students a prompt that will spur controversy, such as:
    ◆ With what event did the author really catch your attention?
    ◆ Did the main character do the right thing?
    ◆ Who is the nicest character?

3. Have students work in small groups to attempt to find a consensus on an answer. Tell them they will need to defend their answer.

4. Have groups share their answers with the whole class, giving solid reasons.

5. Reflect on the experience by asking students, What did it feel like when you were really discussing? What kinds of things did you say and do? Did your thinking change as you were discussing?

STAGE FOUR: SELF-SELECTING TRADE BOOKS TO READ AND DISCUSS

GOAL: To move students toward selecting, reading, and discussing full-length texts

(FOUR TO EIGHT LESSONS)

The overarching goal of literature circles is to create independent, lifelong readers. In order for that to happen students must, at some point, begin to choose their own books. Therefore, we must offer many opportunities to find books they can and want to read.

That's the point of stage four. The teacher creates small groups that each selects its own book, decides how far to read, and chooses a prompt. Students then read independently, respond to the prompt in their journals, and discuss the book in their small groups.

In the first strategy lesson, we discuss ways to spark students' enthusiasm about books. In the second, we show how students can learn to choose books they can read successfully.

Strategy Lesson

BUILDING ENTHUSIASM WITH GOOD READ-ALOUDS AND BOOK TALKS

Sometimes we get students who love to read, but they may be the exception rather than the rule. We suggest two ways to help all students become enthusiastic about books and reading: reading a variety of materials aloud and holding book talks.

READ ALOUD

The books we read aloud should span interests and reading levels. Students can usually comprehend read-aloud books two grade levels above their current grade, so fifth-grade students should be able to follow seventh-grade material comfortably. But we also need to read from picture books with plots that appeal to upper-elementary students, such as the works of Chris Van Allsburg; and chapter books that provide interesting material to discuss, such as *Sleeping Ugly* (Yolen, Coward-McCann). By reading aloud "easy books" like these, the teacher makes it clear that these can provide interesting material for discussion, as well.

BOOK TALKS

This is a fantastic way to get students enthusiastic about choosing books for independent reading and literature circles. Jeni organizes for book talks by gathering several sets of books based on themes of interest to fifth graders, such as courage, family life, and the problems of pre-adolescents. She also includes humor, mystery, realistic fiction, and other genres. (See box on page 51, for a sample book list.) In introducing the books, Jeni describes how each book relates to the life of an average fifth grader and why she likes them. She also reads aloud favorite parts. For example, while introducing *The Trading Game* (Slote, HarperTrophy), Jeni may connect the book's topic, baseball cards, to several students' interest in collecting baseball cards. By making observations and connections like these, Jeni builds student awareness of and enthusiasm for particular books and helps them think through the process of selecting a book for themselves.

Jeni also solicits book testimonials from students. For each book she introduces, she asks for comments from students who have already read it. These testimonials spark the interest of others who might have passed over the book at first glance. (See Chapter 6 for more on helping students gain access to books.)

It is important to allow students to have opinions about books they don't like— and express them without fear of being judged. So Jeni models this kind of response. She acknowledges that there are some books she dislikes and is careful to explain why—the characters' actions aren't realistic, the description of the setting is too long, the language is too flowery, the plot sequence is confusing. Giving students the language to describe their feelings about a story allows them to decide for themselves why a book is or isn't right for them.

Here is a transcript of a book talk led by Jeni. Following the transcript is a description of some strategies for engaging the students.

> **Jeni:** Oh, I only have a few copies of this book (*Cracker Jackson*), but it is by one of my favorite authors, Betsy Byars. She writes a lot of books about children about your ages, and they are all so interesting. I think I like that she makes her characters able to do so many things that people don't expect children to be able to do, like get their parents out of jail or drive a car. If you like, *Cracker*

Jackson is here and so is *The Pinballs*, by Betsy Byars. Has anyone read *Cracker Jackson?*

[Students shake their heads. A few raise their hands.]

Jeni: No? Well, you are in for a treat. Another book we have is *Harriet the Spy*. Raise your hand if you have seen the movie.

[A few students raise their hands.]

Jeni: The book is better. It is hysterical because you get to read right out of her journal. [Reads one of Harriet's outrageous journal entries, a description of her teacher.] Well, she writes all these terrible things in her journal and then if you know the story, what happens to the journal?

Katie: Someone finds it.

Jeni: Yes, someone finds it and it is very funny what happens. Has anyone read the book? Yes, Elaine, what did you think?

Elaine: It was really exciting. And funny.

Jeni: Let's see, we also have *Maniac Magee*. I read this a while ago and to be honest, I can't remember a lot about what happens in it. Can anyone help me?

Caryll: I really liked it, but there were some confusing parts. It wasn't a really funny book, but it did get you thinking about what it would be like to be homeless.

Jeni: I remember getting confused at times, but I really liked the book. Maybe if a group reads this you can remind me of what it was about and see if you get confused too. Here, let me read the back . . .

Leading a book talk is like introducing someone who is about to give a speech. You might not like the person, but you still point out his or her best qualities so audience members can make up their own minds. Sometimes to get kids excited, we have to pretend. For example, when Jeni first took her nephew and niece ice skating, she told telling them how much fun it would be and how lucky they were to go, even though she herself wasn't sure. But her pretended enthusiasm became real. When she told the children how much fun they would have, it became a self-fulfilling prophecy. Enthusiasm for books can work the same way.

Guidelines for Effective, Exciting Book Talks

◆ Share why you like the book. Be specific.

◆ Read the back cover. Pause for dramatic effect.

◆ Read an interesting passage, often the first paragraph of the book.

◆ Share something you know about the author and the types of books he or she writes.

◆ Solicit opinions, both positive and negative, from the students.

◆ Express fascination with the book, but be genuine. It really helps if you love to read.

◆ Give students a reason to read: You can tell me what happens, you can give me your opinion, you can compare this to the movie, you can decide if you agree with your classmates' reviews, you can decide if you like it as much as the author's other book(s).

◆ If you didn't like the book or parts of the book, explain why.

◆ Limit supply to increase demand. ("I only have a few copies.")

STAGE FIVE: PUTTING STUDENTS IN CHARGE

GOAL: To allow students to choose books, organize groups, and conduct discussions independently

(THE REST OF THE YEAR)

In stage five, students become responsible for literature circles, including selecting the book, the section to read each week, and the prompt. Students also have a say in group configurations. Because Jeni does not want member selection to be a traumatic experience, like picking teams, she has students confidentially list several classmates they would like in their group. From those lists, Jeni creates groups in which everyone has at least one good friend.

There are good arguments for both student-created and teacher-created groups. Though Jeni maintains control of the grouping process, she allows student input for two reasons. First, as adults, we almost never find ourselves in a group we don't choose to be in. And when we do find ourselves in such a group, the dynamics are often negative. Second, even as adults we feel more comfortable in a group with at least one good friend. If students know we are trying to make them comfortable, they will be more willing to do their part to make literature circles work.

Next, the groups select a book to read and decide, with input from the teacher, how much they will read each week, and what prompt they will use. They then read the selection independently, respond to the prompt in their journals, and lead their own discussions.

For literature circles, students must be able to read at an independent level. That is, they must be able to read 95 to 100 percent of the words quickly, easily, and accurately (Clay, 1979, 1985). If they are unable to read independently, comprehension breaks down and good discussion becomes impossible. Guided choice and the five-finger method are two ways to encourage children to choose appropriate books:

> **Guided Choice** For the first several literature circle sessions, Jeni gathers books from which the groups could select, including a wide variety of subjects, interest areas, and readability levels. "Easy" books and grade-level books are introduced with equal enthusiasm during book talks.

> **Five-Finger Method** Once children made their choices, she makes sure books are appropriate by applying the five-finger method (Glazer and Brown, 1993). As the student reads aloud a sample passage

Finding the Books You Need

Multiple copies of a single book are essential. Here are some ways to find them:

- Borrow from other classes.

- Purchase multiple copies using PTA money.

- Buy sets through book clubs or use bonus points.

- Get a civic group to donate a set of books.

Great Trade Books for Stage Four and Five Discussions

A Taste of Blackberries
by D. B. Smith (HarperCollins)

Charley Skedaddle
by P. Beatty (William Morrow)

Cracker Jackson
by B. Byars (Penguin Putnam)

From the Mixed-Up Files of Mrs. Basil E. Frankweiler
by E.L. Konigsburg (Simon & Schuster)

Julie of the Wolves
by J.C. George (Harper & Row)

Maniac Magee
by J. Spinelli (Little, Brown)

Mrs. Frisby and the Rats of NIMH
by R.C. O'Brien (Aladdin)

Nothing But the Truth
by Avi (Orchard Books)

Old Yeller
by F. Gipson (Harper & Row)

Roll of Thunder, Hear My Cry
by M. D. Taylor (Puffin Books)

Shiloh
by P.R. Naylor (Dell)

Sing Down the Moon
by S. O'Dell (Houghton Mifflin)

Sounder
by W.H. Armstrong (HarperCollins)

The Midwife's Apprentice
by K. Cushman (HarperCollins)

The Pinballs
by B. Byars (HarperCollins)

The Trading Game
by A. Slote (HarperCollins)

The True Confessions of Charlotte Doyle
by Avi (Avon)

of at least 100 words, count each time he or she is unable to recognize or decode a word. If you count five or more difficult words, the book is below the independent level, and won't work for literature circles. Encourage students to practice the five-finger method regularly on their own.

Ways to Help Students Select a Book They Can Read

◆ Read aloud books that represent a range of reading levels.

◆ Provide a variety of book choices by subject, interest, and readability.

◆ Introduce easy and grade-level books with equal enthusiasm.

◆ Solicit book testimonials from students.

◆ Teach the class the five-finger method for judging a book's readability.

◆ Have children sort books according to factors that make a book easy or difficult.

SORTING BOOKS TO JUDGE DIFFICULTY

Guided choice and the five-finger method are like bicycle training wheels. They help children who have not had much experience riding. We want students to have enough experience with books so that they don't need guided choice or the five-finger method. We want them to choose books based on skimming a passage and determining automatically whether a book is right for them, the way adults choose books.

OBJECTIVE: To help students develop the ability to choose the right books for them independently

MATERIALS: A large selection of books that span difficulty levels, from easy chapter books to middle- and high-school trade books

STEPS:

1. Place students in groups of four to five.

2. Assign students the task of sorting the books by difficulty and creating a list of the books, from easiest to most difficult. Students will need to read at least a paragraph of some books, possibly more of others.

3. At the end of the activity, ask groups to present their lists to the whole class and have them report on how they determined the order. Have them tell if there were disagreements among the group members and why.

4. For the classroom library, ask each student to create a list of three books that are "easy," three that are "difficult," and three or more that are "just right." Label the books according to students' criteria.

Final Thoughts

Susan's experience, described at the start of this chapter, illustrates the importance of time in establishing effective literature circles. Students need time to build trusting relationships with one another before they will take risks. They also need time to become comfortable voicing their point of view and sharing incomplete ideas. And they need time to learn how to exchange ideas in acceptable ways. They need to be assured that the ideas they express will generate a response rather than evaluation. This kind of growth can happen only in a safe environment. All of this takes time.

Time spent allowing students to practice, reflect, try again, make mistakes, and learn from them is time well spent. If literature circles are going to work, you must give yourself and your students the gift of time.

But developing students capable of conducting a rich, thoughtful discussion requires not only time, but also thorough planning, and careful observations to determine when to move students into the next stage. You must be certain that the majority of the class is prepared to proceed before any move is made. Careful attention must be paid to the students' ability to follow guidelines for discussion, use prompts to help focus the discussion, choose appropriate books, and work in small groups.

When Jeni first tried this in her classroom, the plan worked well. We were amazed at the depth of discussion, the students' ability to prepare and organize, and the progress each student made in reading. Literature discussions gave the students an avenue for sharing interpretations and learning from each other.

In these first two chapters we have presented the big picture. The next chapters will provide more details about how to promote good discussion, the role of writing in literature circles, ways to move students toward more sophisticated thinking, techniques for assessment, and strategies for working with those with diverse needs.

CHAPTER 3

Encouraging *Real* Discussion

D iscussion is at the core of literature circles. Without discussion, the reader is confined to only his or her point of view and may not grow in understanding of text, authors, and ideas without having that point of view challenged. Although this is obvious to us, it is not always clear to students. Too often reading in school is a solitary act, either for personal pleasure or as an act of compliance to please the teacher or fulfill an assignment. But over the course of the school year, the students in Jeni's class began to discuss, rather than report, and to respond to one another's ideas, and to broaden their perspectives on books. Reading and thinking about books became a social activity.

In this chapter, we define discussion and show how it differs from other forms of group talk. Next, we explore more deeply the importance of discussion in response to literature. Last, we offer a reality check: We present what we all *hope* goes on in literature circles, what *really* happens, and strategies for moving literature circles toward the ideal.

Discussion:
What It Is and Is Not

DISCUSSION IS SHARED TALK
ABOUT IDEAS

Discussion has a purpose and moves us closer toward the goal of understanding the thoughts of others. In the case of literature circles, it enriches one's own interpretation of what has been read. Ideally, participants in a discussion are open to the ideas of others. After all, there is no point to having a discussion if the participants aren't willing to listen to and consider others' ideas! (Unfortunately, we all know people who seem to think a discussion is just a forum

"What I like is that I get to hear people's opinions and I learn what point of view they think of and how they think and what they're thinking of."

–Bradley

for the presentation of their ideas.) Members of a discussion must be willing to share their ideas with others, too. Those who are not willing to share are at best listeners, but not discussants.

In the excerpt below, Annie, Kate, Sharice, and Carolyn truly have a discussion of *The Pinballs* (Byars, HarperCollins), a book about three foster children. Note how the girls extend each other's comments and elaborate on their topic.

Discussion is shared talk about ideas.

It is goal-directed and purposeful. Discussants are:

◆ open to the ideas of others.

◆ eager to listen and consider new ideas.

◆ willing to share ideas.

Annie: What was the prompt?

Kate: "Describe how you feel about the book."

Annie: I don't like this book.

Sharice: Me either.

Annie: It was all right, I guess. It just doesn't interest me. I mean it was good at the beginning . . .

Carolyn: Yeah.

Annie: But when you got to the end it kind of slowed down and it was . . .

Kate: Yeah.

Annie: The first chapter was really exciting. The third was okay, but it just kind of, it got boring. What do you think about it, Carolyn?

Carolyn: I really like the book. It gives a lot of feeling and emotions. I just really liked it. I mean you can really feel what they're thinking. I mean, what would you feel if your dad like runs over your legs? You wouldn't be able to eat the same things you ate before.

Kate: Like, he didn't eat the chicken but he really wanted it.

DISCUSSION IS NOT JUST CONVERSATION

Conversation is informal talk and is less goal-directed than discussion. Information may be exchanged in a conversation, but it is less likely to be explored, examined, or disputed. Every classroom is filled with conversation (sometimes more than we would like), but true discussion is more rare. For example, the following is a conversation. The girls talk about a topic, but there doesn't seem to be any reason for their exchange of information. The talk might have gone somewhere, but it didn't.

Annie: When was this book made?

Carolyn: It got the award in . . .

Kate: '74

Carolyn: '73, so I think it's an old book.

Kate: Well, the copyright . . .

Annie: 1978

Kate: It's probably a new book, but an old book.

Carolyn: That's what I meant. It must be '73 because it got the children's award.

Kate: Because it was copyrighted in 1973. Do you want to talk about other questions?

DISCUSSION IS NOT REPORTING OR, WORSE, LECTURING

Reporting and lecturing are one-way acts of communication. One person talks, and the others listen and receive information, with no exchange of ideas. If listeners disagree with a report, there is no way to make their differing ideas heard. We have all participated in "discussions" in which one person dominates and clearly is not interested in the ideas of others but only in expounding his or her own thoughts.

In the following excerpt of a discussion of *Baseball Saved Us* (Mochizuki, Lee & Low), Bradley makes a comment. But instead of responding to his idea, Carolyn simply takes her turn and gives her own, unrelated response to the prompt, "Have you ever felt like a character in the book?"

Bradley: Yes, I think I've been in the situation because when I play basketball, everybody thinks I can't play.

Carolyn: I'll go. I don't think I have ever felt like that and so I am very lucky sometimes. If there's someone in my class with a weird name or someone very strange, I might laugh at them but as the year goes on, I find they're not so weird at all, just like in the story.

Clearly Carolyn interprets the task here as "going next" and not responding to the ideas of others.

On the other hand, in this same group, Tanya shows in several ways that she does understand the importance of response. After presenting her own response to the prompt, she asks the group, "Don't you feel like that?" and elicits a response from Sharice. Another example occurs a bit later:

Carolyn: Now what do we do?

Tanya: Don't we talk about the book now?

Carolyn: I don't ever want to feel that way because it would make me feel depressed, because like if some-body would say anything like that to me, it would just make me feel really sad.

Tanya: And then you get real mad at them.

Where Carolyn just reports, Tanya sees the task as following up on others' comments and finding out what everyone thinks.

DISCUSSION IS NOT RECITATION

Too often in classrooms students are asked to recite an answer in response to a teacher's question, and then that answer is evaluated by the teacher. True discussion differs from recitation in important ways. There is no official interrogator. In fact, questions generally arise in literature circles not to "test" whether someone has a particular piece of information but to seek clarification of another's remarks. In a discussion, responses are not assessed for correctness. Instead, members of the group check the ideas of others against their own understandings and then explore differences, not with the idea of finding one right answer but in search of a deeper understanding of the topic. "Right" and "wrong" are less relevant than "richer," "broader," and "deeper."

In this excerpt we return to the discussion of *Baseball Saved Us* from Chapter 1. Three of the students explore the realism of the book by offering their own interpretations of events. Notice that this seems to be a free exchange of ideas, without a sense that the group needs to find the "right" answer.

> **Bradley:** But, I mean if he couldn't hit a ball, that's not that good, I don't think he would really hit a home run all of a sudden.
>
> **Tanya:** You can tell where the book is made up because if he can't hit a ball, how can he make a home run? This doesn't really make any sense.
>
> **Kate:** Actually, he could. They said that he could usually hit base hits, but they thought he was no good because usually he struck out. It's like a fifty-fifty chance that he's going to hit a base hit and strike out and then all of a sudden he just got real mad and he hit it. So in a sense he had so much force that it just went out.
>
> **Bradley:** Well, I don't know. If I was in his place, I don't think that I could've hit a home run with everybody booing at the same time he hit a home run, because that would've really gotten in your mind.

Discussion Is Not:

Conversation, because discussion is goal-directed and conversation is not.

Reporting or lecturing, because discussion is an exchange of ideas and reporting and lecturing are one-way transmittal of ideas.

Recitation, because in discussion there is no questioner who then evaluates answers.

The Importance of
Discussion in Response to Literature

What is it about discussion that is critical to response? Why won't reporting or answering questions, which certainly have been traditional models in classrooms, do just as well in helping children respond to literature? Our goal is to elicit responses that go beyond the surface level of words on the page. We want responses that connect readers to the text in very personal and emotional ways. Four beliefs help us keep that goal in perspective:

- Readers, not authors or teachers, make meaning.
- Meaning-making is personal but grounded in text.
- Literature has multiple interpretations.
- Social interaction is important for response to literature.

READERS, NOT AUTHORS OR TEACHERS, MAKE MEANING

The meaning of a piece of literature is constructed by, built by, created by the reader (Langer, 1992; Rosenblatt, 1978; Short, 1993). Meaning is not just given to the reader by the author, although certainly authors have ideas they would like to give to their readers. Meaning is not given to the reader by people with whom the book is discussed, although the ideas that fly back and forth in discussion surely will help the reader construct his or her personal interpretation. And, to be sure, meaning is not given to the reader by the teacher. Meaning comes from within the reader, not from outside influence.

> **"Meaning is made, not borrowed."**
>
> —Probst, 1981

IMPLICATIONS FOR CLASSROOMS

Occasionally model for the students where your responses come from, so that they can see someone actually constructing meaning. Invite them to share their own constructions of meaning.

Discuss how your interpretation of a piece of literature changed across the story, thus showing that meaning is dynamic, not static. Suggest that students keep logs that show their own changing interpretations of a piece of literature.

Resist the temptation ever to answer the question, "But what is the RIGHT answer?" about the meaning of a piece of literature.

MEANING-MAKING IS PERSONAL, BUT GROUNDED IN TEXT

Because each person makes his or her own meaning from a piece of literature, meaning is personal. But those constructed meanings have some basis in the text. A range of acceptable responses exists, but the range is not unlimited. Response to literature must neither be a search for one right answer nor the acceptance that every idea has value. For example, in the discussion in Chapter 1 about *Baseball Saved Us*, the students did not agree on what the title meant, but no one suggested the book was about the World Series or medical emergencies.

IMPLICATIONS FOR CLASSROOMS

When modeling for the class how you construct meaning, be sure to tell the children that some of your ideas came from the text itself but others came from your own experience. For example: "When I first met Wilbur [of *Charlotte's Web*], I thought he was charming and adorably naïve. He was clueless about why pigs are raised on farms [from text]. But another reason I fell in love quickly with Wilbur is that my neighbor has a Vietnamese potbelly pig, and it is the cutest, smartest little animal I have ever seen. I also loved the pig in the movie *Babe* [from experience]."

Ask the children to tell where their answers come from. This is basically Raphael's Question-Answer Relationships, or QAR (Raphael, 1982), which helps readers understand that their answers might be:

1. Right There (explicitly stated in the text),
2. A product of Think and Search (implicit in the text), or
3. On My Own (from their own experience).

It helps to reassure students at the outset that their answers have merit. Otherwise, when you ask a student to "prove" an answer, too often the automatic response is simply to change the answer. The student thinks you are only asking for proof because the answer is wrong.

LITERATURE HAS MULTIPLE INTERPRETATIONS

If meaning is built by each reader from the text, then clearly different interpretations are to be expected and even celebrated. A reader who has experienced prejudice firsthand and with regularity will respond in different ways to *Roll of Thunder, Hear My Cry* (Taylor, Puffin Books) than one who has merely read about injustice. A reader who has been camping will have different responses to *Hatchet* (Paulsen, Puffin Books) than one whose outdoor experiences have been limited to city life. The first time Dixie heard *Love You Forever* (Munsch, Firefly Books) she burst into tears in the lobby of her school because at that time she was dealing with her mother's deterioration from Alzheimer's. Silverstein's *The Giving Tree* (HarperCollins) has been lauded as an affirmation of the importance of caring for our earth's resources and banned as a religious allegory. We've all been surprised when discussing a book, a movie, or even a news story with a friend to find that a person with whom we share many experiences has an entirely different interpretation.

IMPLICATIONS FOR CLASSROOMS

Model ways to respond positively to interpretations that differ from one's own, such as "Wow! I never thought of Will in that way. What made you think of him like that?"

After a student has provided an interpretation, specifically invite differing interpretations while affirming the response that has already been given. ("Bianca thinks that Carla should have insisted that Saul tell the truth instead of just keeping quiet. I suspect that many of you agree with that. But does anyone have a different opinion? Why?")

SOCIAL INTERACTION IS IMPORTANT FOR RESPONSE TO LITERATURE

This is where discussion comes in. Exposure to the ideas of others during discussion leads to reflection, which leads in turn to revision of meaning, and ultimately to a broader and richer world view. When readers come together to discuss what they have read, they take part in what is called an interpretive community. Through this community, half-formed ideas are explored and readers discover new lenses through which to view what they have read. During a discussion, we have all at one time or another slapped ourselves on the side of the head (literally or metaphorically) with astonishment and said, "I never thought of it that way before!"

Social Interaction and Response to Literature

Discussion with other ⟶ Self-reflection ⟶ Revision of meaning

The social interaction of discussion also helps readers clarify what they think they know and to become aware of how they have come to know (Sheppard, 1990). When we have to explain, we have to understand our own thinking. Even more, Ash suggests that social interaction "brings literature to life: That is the reward of making reading a social affair" (1990, p. 77). Further, discussion often results not just in an airing of individual meanings but in genuine collaboration, which creates something entirely new. Literature discussions can be truly synergistic, with the results being more than the sum of the parts.

IMPLICATIONS FOR CLASSROOMS

Be sure to give ample time for discussion. Accept that there will be some "off-task" social interaction during each gathering. Not every second of our lives needs to be brilliant or proactive.

To increase the students' awareness of how talking with others has affected their own ideas, have students keep "Before and After Logs," where they record their ideas before they discuss and then again after the discussion. (See Chapter 4.)

> "When we invite readers' minds to meet books in our classrooms, we invite the messiness of human response—personal prejudices, personal tastes, personal habits, personal experience. But we also invite personal meaning."
>
> —*Atwell, 1987*

Literature Discussions:
Ideals, Realities, and Solutions

Ideally, literature circles will be forums for dynamic discussions in which students share ideas, respond to each other respectfully, and grow in their understanding of the piece of literature and, indeed, the world itself. That's the ideal we strive for. Reality is a bit different. There are at least three issues that must be addressed to attain this ideal picture:

1. Promoting full participation
2. Creating a risk-free environment
3. Encouraging high levels of thinking

For each issue we will start with the ideal, because teachers have found the ideal is attainable, although it does not spring forth spontaneously and all the issues are rarely resolved exactly as planned. We will tell you about some of the problems teachers encounter and share with you several ways in which we can move students' discussion toward the ideal.

Three Issues
to Address Early and Often

1. PROMOTING FULL PARTICIPATION
THE IDEAL: ALL MEMBERS PARTICIPATE IN THE DISCUSSION

In an ideal discussion group, all members share their ideas and respond to the ideas of others. Of course, we don't expect that all will participate equally, but we would be disappointed if some students dominated their group meeting after

The Issue	The Ideal	The Reality	Some Solutions
Promoting Full Participation	**All members participate in the discussion**	**Participation levels vary widely because:** ◆ some students are dominating, reticent, and/or passive ◆ teacher is controlling the discussion ◆ students are reporting, not discussing ◆ students have difficulty reading the selected book	◆ Plan group membership ◆ Assign roles ◆ Track participation ◆ Use response journals ◆ Make sure the text is accessible ◆ Provide "sub-prompts" ◆ Talk as a class about participation problems
Creating a Risk-Free Environment	**Everyone expresses ideas freely without fear of ridicule**	**Some students do not know how to disagree tactfully. Some may dismiss the ideas of others.**	◆ Model the kinds of responses you expect ◆ Intervene when necessary ◆ Talk as a class about acceptable responses
Encouraging High Levels of Thinking	**All responses are sophisticated and detailed**	**Procedural talk dominates. Students only report. Responses may be shallow or perfunctory.**	◆ Conduct strategy lessons and class meetings ◆ Teach students to dig for answers

meeting, and others rarely spoke. We want turn-taking that shows genuine interest in the ideas of others, and we hope that, if members are not participating, others will attempt to draw them into the discussion. Those who have something to contribute know how to gain the floor, but also know when to give it up to others.

In an ideal group, the students, not the teacher, are in charge of the discussion. The group members set the agenda and resolve conflicts during discussion, whether these conflicts arise from process (how group members are conducting the discussion) or content (what they are saying). And, as a result of the groups being in charge, the students are engaged in the discussion and have a sense of ownership of both the process and the ideas.

When students listen and respond to one another's ideas, they know that what they say matters. They support one another's attempts at making meaning by seeking clarification, expanding on others' comments, and offering alternative interpretations. They see each other as resources for richer understandings, rather than as evaluators of ideas.

THE REALITY: PARTICIPATION LEVELS VARY WIDELY

In reality a group may be far from the ideal. Some students may be dominating, reticent, or passive. The teacher may take over the discussion. Some students may simply report their answers. A few may be unable to read the book and, therefore, have limited opportunities for participation.

But there is also the good news: Students are often able to hold discussions that come close to the ideal, although of course this is not true for all students or in every group meeting. Jeni has found that, in her class, students usually take turns naturally. Often group members notice when someone is not participating and explicitly ask the silent individual to express an opinion. They didn't need to be shown how to do this; they noticed the need and took care of it.

Group facilitators spontaneously emerge in nearly every meeting. Sometimes one person assumes that role in his or her group every time. Kate and Bradley, for example, were natural facilitators who saw the need for a discussion director to keep the group on task, draw out all members, and monitor behavior. Often, different individuals took on the role of facilitator, even within a single meeting.

In the following excerpt, note Kate's persistence in trying to get the discussion started.

Kate: Who wants to go first?

Annie: Carolyn, will you hand me that pillow?

Tanya: I wouldn't [hand her the pillow]. I would tell her to get up and get it herself.

Kate: Who wants to go first?

Sharice: Not me.

Carolyn: I didn't write much.

Annie: I didn't either.

Sharice: I didn't either.

Kate: Do you want to go first, Tanya?

Tanya: Noooo.

Kate: I'll go first. I've never felt like Cracker . . .

But of course leadership does not always emerge smoothly and painlessly. Occasionally attempts at leadership are thwarted, as with Tanya. Because of her often disruptive behavior and poor leadership skills, Tanya was not viewed as a leader by the others in her group when she tried to exert leadership. So when Tanya tried to be the leader, the others usually just ignored her, to her great frustration.

Potential Problem | Some Students Are Dominating, Reticent, and/or Passive

Surprisingly, we have not found that a few students take over every discussion. The "natural leaders" who emerge serve more as facilitators or function to fill a temporary leadership gap. Jeni most often noticed that in her class when one student felt that another was holding the stage longer than he or she should, that person changed the topic or asked another student for an opinion, neatly deflecting attention away from the current speaker. Usually the speaker gracefully gave up the floor.

However, we have observed students who monopolize and direct all interactions. They set the agendas, ask the questions, determine who will respond to questions, and often evaluate the responses of others. Unfortunately it is sometimes easier for the rest of the group to acquiesce. Things move along quickly and the assignment is completed, but discussion frequently suffers.

In Jeni's classroom, we were more worried about the few reticent or passive students than about a few students dominating discussion. For example, when others asked Sharice for her opinion, she frequently didn't answer, giving a shy smile or a gentle shrug of her shoulders. (See Chapter 6 for more on Sharice.)

Such natural reticence is a problem in discussion groups, as is simple passivity. Tanya was, at times, passive. She just didn't tune in. She would stare into space or wander around the room (until Jeni directed her back to the group), and, at those times, was in the meeting in body but clearly not in mind.

Reasons a Text May Not Be Accessible

- The student may not be able to read the words with ease.

- The student may lack background knowledge on the topic.

- The student may have difficulty understanding the structure of the story or literary device.

- The student may have difficulty understanding the vocabulary.

Potential Problem The Teacher Is Controlling the Discussion

Another problem frequently found in literature circles is teacher-centered discussion rather than student-centered discussion. Jeni has avoided that problem simply by not participating as a member of any group, other than as the leader of the initial whole-group discussions. On the rare occasions when Jeni does join a group, she is careful to be "just one of the group." She keeps her eyes down a lot of the time, shuffling papers or looking through the novel, so that the children do not feel they have to address their remarks to her. When she offers comments, they are given as suggestions, preceded by "I wonder if . . .," "It might be that . . .," or "Have you thought about . . . ." By doing this, Jeni sheds her privileged role as teacher in these discussions.

Potential Problem Reporting, Not Discussing

One unanticipated problem emerged in Jeni's class when several groups fell into the habit of reporting rather than discussing. A group would assemble, someone would take charge, and the participants would essentially do round robin reading of their journals. The facilitator would ask Evan to read his journal entry, which he did while everyone listened politely. Then Jenna would be called on to read her entry, and so on. There was no discussion at all. Somehow these students had defined the task as sharing what they had written in their journals and that was all.

Difficulty With the Selected Book
Grouping students based on factors other than reading ability,
such as personality, gender, or friendship patterns, almost ensures heterogeneous
mix of reading abilities. When one book is selected by a group and reading ability
varies across the group, the book is likely to be too easy for some and too hard for
others. If students are reading books that are too difficult or near their frustration
level, they will have a difficult time discussing the book or finding deeper meaning.

Considerations for Placing Students in Groups

◆ Change group membership often so that students can listen to many
  points of view and learn to respect all of their classmates.

◆ Avoid placing students together who do not get along with each
  other.

◆ Experiment with all-girl and all-boy groups in order to ensure that
  girls' voices will be heard.

◆ Once students have experience with literature circles, try letting them
  select their own groups. They are likely to choose individuals with
  whom they get along, thus freeing the group for discussion.

◆ Be particularly careful with struggling students. Place them in groups
  with at least one person who will support them.

SOME SOLUTIONS

We managed to solve problems related to levels of participation in many
different ways. Here are some of our strategies:

Plan Group Membership Problems with group leadership as a barrier to participation are often solved through careful planning of group membership.

Assign Roles Some teachers help to ensure successful group interactions by assigning roles to students on a rotating basis (Daniels, 1994). Thus one week Jenna is the Discussion Director, Ryan is the Vocabulary Enhancer, and DeShawn is the Summarizer. Assigning leadership roles to reticent or passive students can take the stage away from domineering ones. At the next meeting, roles are switched.

We purposely do not assign roles at the beginning because we want to see what roles naturally develop. All in all, we have found that students unconsciously assume roles that are needed and that we do not need to invent roles to make the discussion work. However, many teachers find assigning specific roles an effective temporary step for facilitating discussion.

Track Participation Once students are aware of their own level of participation, changes often occur. So it is a good idea to have them keep track of participation levels. One strategy is to tape a discussion and then have the group listen to the tape, keeping a tally of the number of times each member talks. Another way of keeping a tally is for one person to be assigned the role of Tally Master, responsible for tracking how many turns each person has, and then sharing her or his findings with the group. Another strategy is for the teacher to give each group member a certain number of tokens. Each time a group member offers a comment, he or she puts a token into the middle of the table. When students run out of tokens, they run out of turns and are expected to participate only by listening. Students who use a small number of tokens are encouraged to participate more.

Use Response Journals We find that response journals help ensure that each student comes to the discussion with something to say. (See Chapter 4 for more on the use of journals and prompts.) At the beginning of the year, when everyone is listening to or reading the same short piece of literature, we prescribe a prompt to which all students have to write a response, such as "How were you like the main character?" Later, as we move the students toward independence, each group identifies its own prompt for the next reading assignment, sometimes selected from a list we give them and sometimes created by the group itself. One purpose for using prompts and response journals is to ensure that each student has done some reflection before the group meeting and will be confident that she or he could contribute to the discussion.

Make Sure the Text Is Accessible The piece of literature selected by a group may not be accessible to all members for a variety of reasons. A student may not be able to read the words or have sufficient background knowledge. The story may have an unfamiliar structure or a high level of unfamiliar vocabulary. These problems will interfere with comprehension and, therefore, full participation. Here are some solutions:

◆ **Increase the Students' Awareness of Appropriate Books.**
One way to help ensure that all members of a group can read the selected text is to make sure they have easy access to a wide variety of books.

In her book talks to the class, Jeni is careful to include books at a range of reading levels, including books below the fifth-grade level, so that "easy books" are seen as acceptable to the teacher. In addition, when Jeni reads to the students, she often chooses picture books and other below grade-level materials, to give these books status as potential literature circle selections.

◆ **Use Multiple Books on a Single Theme or Genre.**
Having group members choose themes or genres for their reading, rather than single books, ensures accessible texts for all. A group might choose to read books, on courage or relationships. Or the group might decide to read fairy tales or sport stories. Each member of the group reads a different book at his or her own level and can, therefore, participate in the discussion. Students exploring the theme of valuing yourself and appreciating diversity might choose from books at widely varying levels, such as *Chrysanthemum* (Henkes, Greenwillow Books), *Anastasia Krupnik* (Lowry, Houghton Mifflin), *The Summer of the Swans* (Byars, Viking Press), *Amazing Grace* (Hoffman, Dial Books), *A Bad Case of Stripes* (Shannon, Blue Sky Press), *I Wish I Were a Butterfly* (Howe, Harcourt Brace), and *Stellaluna* (Cannon, Harcourt Brace).

◆ **Bypass Print.**

Another reason students may have problems with a book is that they have difficulty reading the words. Reading books aloud to students is one way to circumvent this problem. Jeni often reads the selected text aloud to two English language learners, Eddy and Juan, and they have been successful in participating in their group discussions. While this strategy does not alleviate reading difficulties at the word level, it permits the students to focus on understanding and interpreting the stories. Word identification strategies are, of course, important, but they should be addressed elsewhere in the literacy program.

The teacher need not be the one who reads the book aloud. Partner reading, where students read aloud to each other, reduces the demands on the teacher's time. Juan and Eddy, the two English-language learners, have successfully used this strategy to supplement Jeni's work with them. Talking word-processing programs, such as *Write: OutLoud*, volume 3 (1999), can also be used, as well as books on tape. Many books are now available in a recorded format and often are available from state departments of public instruction for learning disabled or visually impaired students. Finally, parents or older siblings can read to the children as a homework assignment.

However, we suggest that you use strategies that bypass print sparingly for two reasons. First, such strategies may lead to learned helplessness, whereby the struggling reader learns to depend on an outside source for access to books. Second, unless these strategies are carried out in privacy, which may be difficult, the assisted reader is clearly identified as "not capable."

◆ **Prepare Students to Read the Text.**

Even when students can read the words, books can still be difficult for them to understand for three main reasons. First, children may lack background experiences required for comprehending the book. Imagine trying to read and discuss a textbook on statistics without ever having had a course in the subject. Second, readers can also have difficulty understanding a book when the author uses a structure or literary device that students are unfamiliar with, such as flashbacks. Finally, the vocabulary the author uses may be unfamiliar to the students.

These issues are not mutually exclusive. If a book addresses an unfamiliar topic, for example, chances are it contains vocabulary unfamiliar to the students, as well.

When these types of problems arise, strategy lessons can help. For example, Jeni once noticed that one group, which had chosen *The Midwife's Apprentice* (Cushman, HarperCollins), was having a particularly difficult time. The first thing that Jeni did was try to figure out the source of the problem. She listened in on the group's discussion and asked students who seem to be in trouble to read a passage from the book aloud and describe the story. This helped determine whether they were having difficulty reading the words, problems with vocabulary, confusion over the plot line, or a combination of the three.

Through her eavesdropping, Jeni learned that the students were having a hard time identifying with the main character because of the historical context. So she provided a strategy lesson focused on making the book relevant by comparing the feelings and circumstances of the medieval main character and the feelings and circumstances of students today. After the strategy lesson, students were more able to make their own personal connections with the story and were able to discuss it.

Strategy Lesson

DEEPENING STUDENTS' CONNECTIONS TO CHARACTERS

OBJECTIVE: To enrich students' comprehension of a story by showing them how to relate their own experiences and feelings to a character's experiences and feelings

STEPS:

1. Identify whether students are having difficulties comprehending the book by eavesdropping on the group's discussion or questioning the individual members.

2. Compare the character's experiences and feelings to your own. For example, during a discussion of *The Midwife's Apprentice*, Jeni said that the main character must have felt "desperate" when she had to sleep in cow manure to keep warm. She then described one situation where she had once felt desperate.

3. Solicit comparisons between the students' lives and the main character's life. After Jeni provided her comparison, she asked for situations in which students had felt "desperate," and they were all able to relate stories of feeling this way.

4. Continue providing and soliciting comparisons until the students appear to be relating to the circumstances of the main characters—and other characters.

If students find it hard to follow the plot line, provide a visual representation of the story, such as a time line, plot diagram, or character map. Students can also be taught to untangle stories as they go by developing their own visual representations of the relationships among story events.

Provide "Probes" When we notice that students do not respond to one another's comments, and instead just make another comment on the same topic, Jeni provides a strategy lesson on "probing." The class developed a list of probes, or sub-prompts, that can be used to expand discussion. (See Chapter 4 for more on using probes.)

Talk as a Class About Participation Problems The last way we attempt to address problems with participation is through whole-group debriefings. Whatever the problem, we find that a class discussion helps the students clarify the nature of the difficulty and engages them in finding solutions. For example, when we decide to move from teacher-selected to student-selected

Sample Probes for the Prompt "Would You Read Another Book by This Author?"

◆ What were your favorite parts?

◆ What did those parts have in common?

◆ Did you like the main character?

◆ Did you care what happened to him or her?

groups, we hold a meeting to discuss what might be the criteria for a good group. The class generally concludes that, although you certainly would want to be with people you like, you don't necessarily want to pick your best friends. They discuss criteria such as shared interests, ability to get along with each other, being able to read the same level of books, and even gender. Jeni then asks students to list privately anyone they really want to have in their group and, if necessary, anyone they would prefer not to have in their group.

The class meeting simplified Jeni's task of sorting out requests because the children take everything that is discussed into account. As a result, she is able to form groups that both meet the students' wishes and make sense to her from the point of view of classroom dynamics.

2. CREATING A RISK-FREE ENVIRONMENT
THE IDEAL: EVERYONE EXPRESSES IDEAS FREELY WITHOUT FEAR OF RIDICULE

In order for students to express their ideas freely, they must trust the members of their discussion group. They have to be confident that they can try out half-formed ideas without being ridiculed and express uncertainties without being labeled "stupid." They must know that they can disagree with another's ideas without being viewed as negative or non-supportive. They have to trust that the members of their group will actually listen to their ideas respectfully and with genuine interest.

Group members understand they do not have to come to consensus in their discussions. When students develop a tolerance for, and even an expectation of, ambiguity and the need to frequently re-think their ideas, they are more likely to risk suggesting alternate points of view and changing their own minds.

Last of all, in a risk-free environment students know how to facilitate discussions, not control them. When they know how to solve conflicts through negotiation rather than through intimidation, abuse, withdrawal, or appeal to the teacher, they do not attempt to avoid conflict or disagreement. They recognize disagreement as an inevitable outcome of the personal nature of response to literature, and are comfortable with it.

THE REALITY: SOME STUDENTS DO NOT KNOW HOW TO DISAGREE TACTFULLY. SOME MAY DISMISS OTHERS' IDEAS.

Jeni provides a safe environment for students by accepting ideas, listening attentively, treating ideas as tentative, and not accepting unkindness. Although it is uncommon, she still occasionally has a student who disagrees tactlessly. She also has students who dismiss the ideas of their classmates. This most often happens to students of low status (social or academic) or those who are out of favor with the group for some reason. Tanya often found her ideas completely disregarded after she had been disruptive or uncooperative. The other girls in her group routinely ignored Tanya's disruptions, but they also ignored her contributions. Here, in a discussion of *The Pinballs* (Byars, HarperCollins), Tanya makes an important point, which is completely ignored by the others:

Carolyn: I kind of felt alone, sometimes just because, like my family would make decisions and they wouldn't like let me in on them, like with the cat's name.

Kate: Well, that's different from Carly or Joey [characters in the book who are in foster care].

Tanya: But they're not really family. They're like close friends. They're not really family, you know, by law, but . . .

Kate (interrupting): Sharice, would you like to go?

SOME SOLUTIONS

Although this class was essentially a kind group of kids who were usually careful of each other's feelings, we took some specific steps to create a risk-free environment. The following strategies will also be helpful to children who are less sensitive in interacting with their classmates.

Model the Kinds of Responses You Expect Jeni consistently stresses two points in formal and informal settings:

1. **It is all right to disagree with your teacher and with others, because that often means you are thinking.**

   Typical comments Jeni makes throughout the day:

   - "My own opinion is. . . . Does anyone else have a different opinion?"
   - "I have just made an outrageous remark. Do you all agree with what I said?"
   - "Annie has just expressed one point of view. Does anyone look at this in another way?"

2. **When you do disagree, or when your teacher disagrees with you, there are ways to do so that are more appropriate than others.**

   Typical comments Jeni makes throughout the day:

   - "Bradley has just said, 'I never thought about the issue in that way. The way I thought about it was....'"
   - "I really disagree with what you just said because [give reasons]."
   - "I think you may have forgotten to consider . . ."
   - "Earlier today I heard someone disagree by telling the other person that he was stupid to think thus and so. How can we tell someone we disagree without calling them names or making them angry?"

Intervene When Necessary Jeni also directly intervenes as needed, as when we discovered that Bradley's all-male group consistently turned off the tape recorder, which was being used for tracking participation, whenever they disagreed. Whenever they actually had a real discussion with different opinions being expressed, they thought something bad was happening and didn't want Jeni to know about it! Once we noticed this behavior, Jeni reviewed the reasons why disagreements should occur and explicitly forbade the boys to turn the recorder off.

If she observes a group's behavior deteriorating, Jeni takes it as a signal that it might be time to reconfigure the groups. And, of course, she sometimes has to remove a student from a group for a temporary time-out.

Talk as a Class About Acceptable Responses Jeni also holds class meetings to discuss the issues and find solutions.

DISAGREEING AGREEABLY

OBJECTIVE: To help students disagree in a way that will promote, rather than hamper, discussion

MATERIALS: A blank chart for each student, chart paper, and markers

STEPS:

1. Present the problem of disagreeing insensitively to the students.

2. Have a student act out a scene with you in which the student disagrees with you in an insensitive way and you simply stop talking. Ask the class to identify the problem.

3. Ask the students to share times when their feelings have been hurt when someone disagreed with them. Be sure to warn them to avoid using anyone's real name in describing these situations.

4. Lead the children to the understanding that disagreeable ways of disagreeing shut down discussion, and that is bad for literature circles.

5. Try some role playing as a follow-up. Have the class do "thumbs up" or "thumbs down" to indicate whether the role player is using a good or bad strategy.

6. Follow up by having students collect data on disagreements and create a chart like this:

How the person disagreed	How the other person reacted	Was this a good or bad way to disagree?
That's dumb!	She got mad and quit.	Bad because they didn't talk any more.
I don't agree, but let's keep going anyway.	He shrugged and said "okay."	Good because they didn't fight.
I wish you weren't so bossy. You never like my ideas.	She said, "But your ideas stink!"	Bad because now they hate each other.

7. Have students meet to share findings in small groups that are different from their literature circles.

8. Bring the whole class together and discuss the kinds of "bad" ways to disagree and what happens when people disagree in those ways.

9. Make and post a class chart of good ways to disagree.

Throughout the day, look for opportunities to celebrate use of "good" strategies. Catch students being "good." At the same time, step in as needed for a private discussion with someone who is having particular difficulty with disagreeing agreeably.

3. ENCOURAGING HIGH LEVELS OF THINKING
THE IDEAL: ALL RESPONSES ARE SOPHISTICATED AND DETAILED

When students talk regularly about what they read, their responses to literature are likely to become more sophisticated and substantive. They become more critical readers. (See Chapter 4 for more about stretching children's thinking.) They learn to state their ideas clearly. Discussion forces more explicit thinking

and an awareness of what in the text triggered a particular response. Students learn
to relate what they read to their own lives.

THE REALITY: PROCEDURAL TALK DOMINATES. STUDENTS ONLY REPORT. RESPONSES MAY BE SHALLOW OR PERFUNCTORY.

Our experiences with Jeni's fifth-grade class showed that students are capable of

---

Two Discussions That Show Higher-Level Thinking

Discussion 1

Bradley: How would you change the book?

Jared: If I was the author, I would change the book and make it much longer and make the guards chase the thief and make the queen chase the guy that chased her off the cliff.

Bradley: I would change the story and add more detail and make the girl fight and throw the man off the cliff.

Jared: I would make the story longer. And would make the girl good-looking! I would make the pictures better because the story is a little dull.

Discussion 2

James: Do you think Charley Skedaddle had a choice to join the gang?

Bradley: I think he had a choice. He was a strong kid and he could do it, but I don't think he should have joined the gang. But it did make the book interesting because he was in the gang and then went in the army. Probably it made him a better fighter in the army.

Jared: I don't think he should have joined the gang. He's too small. I think he should join the army and he could learn more from the army about fighting instead of from the streets.

---

higher level thinking. We were delighted to find that the students often relate what they read to their own lives, interpreting stories in light of their own experiences, comparing interpretations, and challenging authors' decisions. When asked which character he'd like to be in a story, James replied that he'd like to be the big brother "because I'd get to boss my little brother around all the time." And Kate responded to the prompt "Have you ever felt like the main character?" by making a link to her own life, saying, "Sometimes I'm determined to do stuff like stand up to my brothers."

These examples show the depth of response of which children are capable. But don't be misled. Many discussions, both at the beginning of the year and at the end, have only flashes of such brilliance. Often discussion is dominated by procedural talk ("Who wants to read the prompt?" "Did you say your name into the recorder?" "How far were we supposed to read?"). At other times participants report but do not discuss. So, even though an individual student might present a provocative or mature response, that response may not provoke discussion. Rather, another group member is likely to make an unrelated comment that leads the discussion in a different direction.

Some responses, of course, will be shallow. For example, students are often unable to go beyond the literal when responding to the prompt "Have you ever felt like the character?" James replied, "I've never felt like this character because I've never been in problems with gangs, and my brother's never been killed and I never had problems with the army."

Students will also provide perfunctory responses, obviously for the purpose of having something written in their journals just to get the task done. It is not unusual to find journal entries such as "I like this book" or "I would not read another book by this author," but with no elaboration.

Other teachers report receiving summaries of what was read which seem designed merely to prove that the student has done the assignment, much like the classic book report.

SOME SOLUTIONS

Conduct Strategy Lessons and Class Meetings When problems are encountered, Jeni either holds a class meeting or provides a strategy lesson. We almost always find that students take these discussions to heart and put the new strategies into use. When Jeni felt that group discussion of the prompt "Have you ever felt like this character?" was somewhat superficial, for example, she provided a quick strategy lesson on how to respond to that prompt when the reader isn't exactly like the person in the book.

Teach Students to Dig for Answers: Jeni often finds that in-depth discussions do not develop because students wander from topic to topic. To extend discussions, she teaches students to probe the answers to the prompts that students provide. First, she provides the students with the probes shown in Chapter 4. Then she provides a strategy lesson on focusing and extending discussion.

Strategy Lesson

FOCUSING AND EXTENDING DISCUSSION

OBJECTIVE: To assist students in focusing so that multiple responses are made to one topic, thus encouraging more sophisticated and in-depth discussion

MATERIALS: A short story to read to the class, a prompt to go with the story, and chart paper

STEPS:

1. Present the problem. Say something like: "I have noticed that sometimes your discussions wander all over the place. One person might ask, 'What did you like most or least about this story?' and one or two people might respond. Then right away someone asks a different question."

2. Help the class understand why this is a problem. "Although you are asking great questions and using thought-provoking prompts, you don't spend enough time exploring the answers. It's almost as if asking a good question is all there is to a discussion. Certainly discussions are better if good prompts are used, but the reason you ask good questions in the first place is to get some good discussion going."

3. Brainstorm solutions. Possible responses:
   ◆ Ask a question or provide a prompt such as "Would you read another book by this author?" and then don't ask another question until everyone has responded at least once to that question.
   ◆ Don't use more than two main prompts in a discussion. Instead, use probes to extend answers, so that people have to explain their ideas thoroughly. (See Chapter 4 for a complete list of probes.)

4. Practice using the solutions in a mock discussion. Say something like: "Let's try two of these solutions. We will ask Tara's group to come to the front of the room and try to follow our solutions. I am going to read you a short story. I think these two prompts will help us have an interesting discussion." Share with students the prompts you have chosen and read aloud the short story. In small groups, have students respond to the prompt.

5. Reflect on how the groups did as a class. Say something like: "How did your groups do? How did you make sure that everyone responded to the first prompt? How did you make sure that they didn't wander all over in their discussion? Is there anything you might have done even better?"

6. Summarize and post the solutions. Say something like: "We have come up with strategies to help us focus our discussions. I will put these strategies on the wall. The next time your literature circle meets, I want you to do two things. First, review the strategies. Second, put one person in charge to remind you to follow the strategies."

The key to solving nearly every problem is to identify it, discuss it as a whole class, and brainstorm ways to overcome it together. Sometimes the class will suggest a good solution and sometimes you must provide it.

Final Thoughts

Most students are excited about participating in literature circles and are able to do so with high levels of sophistication. But not every day, and not in every way. Over the course of the school year we try things out, celebrate breakthroughs, tinker with problems, and learn. In Chapter 4 we show how one particular strategy, using writing, is an integral aspect of helping students grow in the intensity and depth of their responses to literature.

Writing and Thinking
in Response to
Literature Circles

While we often think of writing as a means of communication or expression, writing is also a tool—one we use every day. We use it to help remember (grocery lists, ideas for birthday gifts, journals), to plan (calendars, budgets, lists of things to do), to analyze (lists of pros and cons about taking on a new opportunity), and to share thoughts (letters and e-mails). Often, as we express our thinking on paper, we clarify our thoughts or think about things in new ways, such as writing this book, or writing a letter explaining a decision, or trying to persuade someone to do something.

One spring day during the whole-group debriefing session, several students in Jeni's class expressed frustration with students interrupting during literature circles and suggested that writing might be a tool to help solve the problem. Here is a transcript of that session.

Jeni: Some students have told me they were frustrated today. Can you tell me what happened, A.J.?

A.J.: Group members always interrupt me and I don't get to finish what I am saying.

Katie: I talk about what I am thinking and then other group members don't listen, they just say what they were going to say anyway.

Jeni: What should we do?

A.J.: Students who interrupt should lose points.

Katie: Yeah!

Jeni: Taking away points is sometimes a way to help people remember if they have developed a bad habit. My mom used to charge us a quarter if we forgot our chores. Sometimes, knowing you will lose a quarter helps you remember to do your chores. I think that first, though, we should think about the problem some more. Why do you suppose that people interrupt? I sometimes interrupt others, and I think we all do sometimes. Why do we do that?

Adele: I do sometimes when I have something very important to say.

Tracey: I interrupt when I think I am going to forget what I am going to say.

Jeni: Wow. That makes sense to me. I know I don't like to forget what I want to say. And it made me think of something else. I think I also interrupt when I feel very strongly about something. It's not a good habit but it's hard to not do. However, you gave me a good idea. Maybe we should figure out what to do if we think we are going to forget what we are going to say but we also want to listen to others. Does anyone have any ideas?

Adele: Maybe we could bring our journals and make notes during the conversation so we don't forget.

A.J.: I like that idea, unless people are writing and not listening.

Jeni: Do you want to try that and see how it goes? Be prepared to share at our next whole-class share what groups tried that and how it went.

This was one of the first times Jeni noticed her students suggesting that they use writing as a tool to help them remember what they want to say and to make the conversation flow.

In literature circles, writing is an important tool. The purpose of this chapter is to look at writing in literature circles from several different perspectives. First we describe how writing enhances discussion. Next we describe one kind of writing we use with our groups—journals—and give examples of the kinds of writing and thinking that take place with journal writing. Third we talk about responding to writing. Finally, we provide several strategy lessons to help students think more deeply about text through writing.

The Value of Writing
Before and After Literature Circles

Writing helps students become aware of their responses and think more deeply about what they are reading. It helps them capture and reflect on their initial reactions. This heightened interaction with literature is important because the success of literature circles depends on the extent to which students think about what they read. Writing also allows students to reflect on their own experiences within literature discussions. Writing and talking also support one another: by writing, students talk more, and by talking, students write more.

There are many other benefits of writing. We know that when students write about what they read, particularly their responses to their reading, they remember more and can analyze and synthesize what they read, rather than merely recall. We also know that students gain more from composing their thoughts than from writing answers to short or fill-in-the-blank questions. For more on how writing helps children think, see Judith Langer's *How Writing Shapes Thinking*.

Writing in a journal before literature circle sessions makes discussion progress more smoothly. Pre-writing is less stressful than sharing one's thoughts orally because it allows students time and space to think. When students are writing, they can pause, gather their thoughts, revise their responses, and try out risky ideas all within the privacy of the page and in an unhurried manner. Once discussion begins, privacy decreases, risks increase, and the pace picks up. In addition, pre-writing gives discussions a place to start, because students have already considered their responses to the book and have thought of something to say. Pre-writing also gives the teacher information since responses can be used to assess what students understand and to plan instruction.

How Writing Benefits Literature Circles

- Students remember more about what they read than they might with discussion alone.

- Students spend more time reflecting on their reading than they might with discussion alone.

- Students analyze and synthesize what they read more easily.

- Students respond in a safe, non-judgmental environment.

- Students have a place to begin their discussion.

- Students share their thoughts with the teacher and, in doing so, provide a basis for assessment.

KEEPING WRITING INFORMAL

We want students' written responses to be informal so they are more willing to take risks. It is important, therefore, to let them know that this writing will be primarily assessed for ideas, rather than grammar and mechanics. Think about when you use your own writing as a tool. When you make a list, it is important that it be neat and readable, but very few of us create second and third drafts of our grocery lists or our journals. If this writing is graded for grammar and mechanics, students may begin to care more about the form of their writing than the ideas involved, and will not see it as something helpful, which defeats the purpose. Polished work is important, but for other parts of the curriculum.

Kinds of Journal Entries

We recommend having students keep response journals. Jeni has students write two journal entries for each literature discussion, one before the discussion and one after.

PRE-DISCUSSION ENTRY

The first journal entry, assigned the previous week to prepare for the discussion, is based on a prompt the group chooses or one that the teacher assigns. This initial entry is not limited to the prompt and might address anything the students want to discuss about the reading.

This first entry is a chance for students to think on their own about the text. It gives you a sense of how well they are comprehending, what types of analytical abilities they are developing, what prompts they prefer, and how much effort they are putting into preparing for literature circles.

It also gives an idea of what students are getting from the text on their own and if the books they are choosing are at the appropriate level. When one student in Jeni's class wrote this response, it indicated he might not understand the reading:

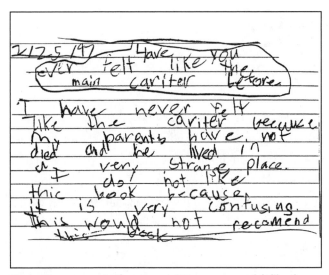

Student's response to the prompt, "Have you ever felt like the main character before?"

Jeni questioned him about the book and found the text was far too difficult. This information prompted her to find something that every student in the group could read successfully.

Olga Dysthe looked at formal and informal responses to literature and found that children who wrote informally to help them prepare for class discussions began to use writing as a tool, often writing when they weren't asked to because they were aware of how writing helped them. Because writing didn't have to be perfect, the children were comfortable using it to help them think through their ideas. This was especially true for the lowest ability students, those least likely to participate in class, because informal writing was so much less threatening to them than formal writing.

—Dysthe, 1996

POST-DISCUSSION ENTRY

The second entry, written as a follow-up to the discussion, helps students reflect on their discussion by answering questions like these: Did your opinions change? Did you understand anything better after the discussion? How did your discussion go? Did your group have interesting things to say?

The second entry lets students elaborate on answers and incorporate new ideas they may have from the discussion. It also gives students a forum for sharing problems and concerns with their teacher that they may not feel comfortable sharing with the whole class. These entries help Jeni see what types of things students get from discussion, how their opinions change, and how literature circles influence their thinking. For a sample journal entry form, see Appendix A.

Two Examples
of Students' Responses

Journal excerpts from two students in Jeni's class show how discussion deepens from before to after and illustrate how writing and discussion enrich one another. The students are in the same discussion group, reflecting on the prompt "Have you ever felt like the main character?" One student is a strong reader and writer; the other is less successful. The story, *A Promise to the Sun* (Mollel, Little Brown), is a fable about a bat who makes a promise that he cannot keep because the birds, friends that he depended on, deserted him.

LUCY'S JOURNAL

Lucy was one of the more successful students in the class.

> **First entry, before discussion:** *Yes, I have felt like the birds before. Someone asked me to do something and I put it off 'til later. I've also felt like the bat. Making a promise and breaking it and feeling real bad. Also feeling like I have to do something by myself and feeling like can't and won't be able to do it.*

> Entry #1   Have you ever felt like   1-21-97
> a character in the story?
>
> Yes, I have felt like the birds before.
> Someone asked me to do something and
> I put it off 'til later. I've also felt
> like the bat. Making a promise and
> breaking it and feeling real bad. Also
> feeling like I have to do something
> by myself and feeling like can't and
> won't be able to do it.
>
> After   My group didn't have much to say
> BC   about feeling like other characters.
> But one thing Ashley said caught
> my attention. She said that she had
> felt like the bat by having such a
> big responsibility and now that I
> think about it the bat had a lot
> on her hands and if I had that
> much to do I'd be stressed out too.

Lucy's original pre- and post-discussion entries

Sharice's original pre- and post-discussion entries

> A Promise to the sun   1-21-97
>   Before
> Yes I felt like a carter in the story.
> I felt like the bat when he said:
>   Earth has no rain,
>   Earth has no food,
>   Earth aks for rain!
>
> and I felt like the bird. I don't Know
> why.
>
>   After
> I would not read this book over
> agin. It would be for a little
> kid. I felt like the main
> Charter. I felt like th main Charter
> because I was in a club & we
> made a promise to the teacher
> that we will keep the club togather
> but we didn't.

Second entry, after discussion:

My group didn't have much to say about feeling like other characters. But one thing Ashley said caught my attention. She said that she had felt like the bat by having such a big responsibility and now that I think about it the bat had a lot on her hands and if I had that much to do, I'd be stressed out too.

SHARICE'S JOURNAL

Sharice was a student who struggled in the class.

First entry, before discussion: *Yes I felt like a charter [character] in the story. I felt like the bat when he said:*

> *"Earth has not rain,*
> *Earth has no food,*
> *Earth asks for rain!"*

And I felt like the bird. I don't know why.

Second entry, after discussion: *I would not read this book over agin. It would be for a little kid. I felt like the main charter. I felt like the main charter because I was in a club and we made a promise to the teacher that we will keep the club together but we didn't.*

Although these entries were from early in the year, there are clear signs of literature circles' positive impact on students' talking and writing. Both students show evidence of the discussion in their thinking afterwards. Lucy, the more successful student, can put herself in the character's position and relate to him on both a superficial ("I've done that before") and an emotional ("I've felt like that before") level. After discussion, however, she still sees the book differently based on Ashley's response. She's developed empathy for the main character, the bat, by thinking about what he might have been feeling. Rather than seeing herself as smarter than other students, Lucy works to learn from them, because while children come with different abilities, they also come with a wealth of experiences that help them think about books differently. While Lucy had a strong sense of responsibility, Ashley had a strong sense of empathy, and both perspectives were relevant to understanding of the main character's experiences.

Sharice, the less successful student, understands that she should compare herself to a character, but initially doesn't seem to have a sense of what that means. After discussion, however, she is able to relate an event in her life that is similar to a situation a character experienced, showing that the discussion increased her understanding of the task as well as her connection to the book. Sharice is able to compare herself on at least a superficial level to the main character by finding a shared experience. We've found that initial steps like these lead to deeper understandings of and connections to a book.

It became clear through the writing, that, as students talk about their ideas, those ideas grow richer, strengthening our belief in mixed-ability grouping. Students who are able to see and find connections help those who aren't. We also find it is not always the high-ability readers who are able to make the most interesting connections or sustain the discussion. For example, it was Tanya, a moderately successful student, not one of the three girls identified as academically gifted, who said while reading *The Pinballs* (Byars, HarperCollins), the tale of children struggling to survive within a foster-care system, "These kids need a savior."

Responding
to Students' Writing

When students respond to each other's writing, as when journal entries are shared in literature circles, it gives the writing a purpose and an audience, two things that motivate students to write more.

But for the writing to have maximum impact, the teacher must also respond to it on a regular basis. When teachers talk to students about their writing or put responses in the margins, student motivation increases. The journals also provide a place for the teacher to enter the discussion. Jeni does not join in discussions, as a general rule, unless there is a clear reason for doing so. By responding to students' ideas in the journals, however, she is able to be a part of the discussion while not taking it over. By writing back and forth, she can also build relationships with students that she often doesn't have time for during the busy school day.

OFFERING RESPONSES THAT LEAD TO MORE REFLECTIVE WRITING

When Jeni reviews journal entries, she usually looks for two parts: (1) An opinion or statement and (2) reasons to back it up. Often students are able to form an opinion ("It was interesting, exciting . . ."), but they are less able to back it up with reasons or examples. Take Alan's entry, for example, on page 95.

Vocabulary is often an issue. Sometimes students don't have the words to form an opinion of their book. Therefore, we need to model how we talk about books, so that students can learn to apply that knowledge. We also need to help children focus on backing up their opinions with details and reasons. To do that, we make sure that our responses usually contain four elements:

- ◆ A reaction, usually an empathetic comment that notes similarities and differences between teacher and student ideas.

- ◆ A note about what good readers do or think when they read.

- ◆ A synonym for overused words, such as "interesting" and "exciting," to stretch vocabulary.

- ◆ A question or challenge that encourages the student to develop well-formed opinions.

Here is an early entry for Ryan. He gives several opinions but doesn't back them up with reasons. Jeni's comments center around giving Ryan synonyms for "interesting" and getting him to elaborate on "good description."

> I think that charley is the most infrastresting criacter in this book because he is the main chapter I liked this book because it is a good adventor this is a very good book because it has a lot of good discription.
>
> Ryan
> I like adventures a lot too. I like a lot of interesting things to happen to the characters and lots of action because you feel like you are a part of it all. When you read you get to have the adventures with the characters.
>
> I don't know what you mean by "good description." Do you mean how she describes what is happening? What does she say to make you feel like you are there? Help me understand.
>
> Mrs. Day

MANAGING YOUR RESPONSE TIME

Responding to journals can be an overwhelming task, so consider reviewing only about quarter of the total each day. That way, by the week's end, you will have looked at all the journals. Weekly review is especially important at the beginning of the year, when students are new to writing entries. As they become more skilled, and are truly using their journals as tools for thinking, you can move to every other week or every three weeks, reviewing a half or a third of the journals weekly.

Jeni finds it interesting to collect and read all of the journals from one group at the same time, in order to see how different students respond to the same text and how the conversation influences entries.

June 20, 1997

I think the book is boring so far and I think he should'nt sell a Ace card for that I woud sell if for a hole lot more. He should take that hole set that the boy that has block deal.

Here, Evan has given an opinion and reasons for his opinion. To push him further, Jeni wants to encourage him to think about another point of view. Why did the author make the choices she did? She wants him thinking about the problem from more than one angle.

Evan

I understand how you feel Its hard for me to enjoy a book when I don't undelstand or agree with what the main character is doing.

Why do you suppose the author had the boy hesitate to trade his baseball card? Wouldn't it change the ending too much if he did? How would the author build suspense Then?

Mrs. Day

4/8/97 What do you think of the book So Far

The book seems exciting so far. There were a lot of events that made it exciting. One of those parts was when Checker was hiding in the bushes at his X-babysitter's house when her boyfriend wasn't there and then her boyfriend drove up unexpectedly.

This response was written toward the middle of the year. Alan has developed an opinion ("the book is exciting") and has given an example from the text to back it up. To push Alan further, Jeni wants to help him take apart text and think about how the author creates excitement.

Alan

I really like how The author builds suspense too. You can hardly stop reading.

I've been trying to figure out how she does that so well and I wonder if its because she uses such great action verbs. When you read the next chapter, think about that and let me know

Mrs. Day

KEEPING WRITING GOING THROUGHOUT THE YEAR

While students are generally willing to write entries at the beginning of the year, it is easy for them to lose steam and put only a perfunctory amount of time into their journals as the year progresses. Moving them beyond superficial thinking is a continuous process. Several ways we found to help students think more deeply about the text include using prompts; helping students wonder, notice, and question; and teaching questioning skills.

Prompts:
The Key to Helping Students Think More Deeply

While we want students to attend to what really strikes them or stays with them as they read, asking them to just "talk about" the book isn't enough. That's why we use prompts to help students respond, question, and theorize about what they have read. A good prompt can be used with any book to provide a way to think about the text and ground students' writing.

For students who do not respond deeply to literature, prompts can move them away from summarizing: "My book was about a girl who was named Beetle, she was poor and didn't have parents and one day she met a midwife who offered her a place to stay so she decided to stay with her . . . ."

Prompts are also helpful if a group of students has had experience discussing literature but misunderstand the concept of response as a free-for-all where anything is fine to talk about: "The character in this story traveled to Mexico. I went to Mexico on a vacation with my family, too, and we had a great time. We saw the beach and went diving and shopping." While we want children to connect the experiences of characters in books to their own experiences, we want to move them further along and encourage them to use their experiences to better understand the story and the characters' experiences.

The goal of using prompts is to jump-start thinking—and then move students along from them before they become dependent on them. Jeni frequently asks students to share experiences of how their groups began with a prompt but then moved beyond. For example, one group discussing *The BFG* (Dahl, Farrar, Straus and Giroux) began with "Would you read another book by this author?" and ended up discussing the merits of reading realistic fiction versus humor. Another example is a group that began discussing if they were like the title character in *Cracker Jackson* (Byars, Penguin Putnam) and ending up discussing whether they would have done what Cracker did when he tried to rescue a friend without alerting the police.

Jeni also uses class discussions for reflecting on how prompts help the group think, what the prompt did for discussions, and how to move beyond a prompt. She also has groups share a favorite prompt, one that has led to interesting discussion. Jeni always lets students know that they can and should move beyond the prompt in discussion and recognizes instances of when they do so.

Strategy Lesson   PROBING A TEXT

One day, while listening in on literature circles, Jeni overheard Laura read her journal response to the prompt "Are you alike or different from one of the characters?" for *The Midwife's Apprentice* (Cushman, HarperCollins). She read, "I am nothing like the midwife's apprentice because I knew my name in the beginning and I was never an orphan." This response concerned Jeni. Although Laura was answering the prompt, she was relating the character to herself only on a superficial level. Laura's response did not help her see the connections she *did* have with a character who lived 800 years ago under very different circumstances. We want students to find similarities and differences between themselves and book characters so they can understand the characters better. Our enjoyment of books often hinges on whether we connect with characters' inner struggles and circumstances. But many of Jeni's students see only surface similarities and differences.

Because Jeni was concerned, she joined the group and listened as two other students shared similarly disappointing journal entries. She asked them to describe

Prompts
for Different Purposes

MAKING PERSONAL CONNECTIONS

- What did the story remind you of?
- Tell about at least one connection that you can make personally with the characters or story. Do you have some shared interest, feeling, or experience? Are you like or different from one of the characters?
- What kind of reader would like this book?
- Is there any character in this story/book like you? How is this character like you?
- Is there a character in this story/book who would make a good friend?
- Compare at least two characters to yourself, your family, or your friends.

IDENTIFYING IMPORTANT ELEMENTS

- What are one or two of the most important ideas from this story?
- What was the author trying to tell you about life with this story?
- What do you think was the most important or most interesting part of this story?
- Who do you think was the most important character? Why was this character important?
- As you get into your novel, you should get to know the main character. Describe the person physically, but also give examples of how she or he feels and what she or he does.
- Choose a character in the book who is important but not the main character. Describe this person, explain her or his relationship to the main character, and tell why she or he is important in the story.
- What surprised you in this story? Why was that a surprise? What did you expect instead?
- Does the title fit the story? Why or why not?

Prompts
for Different Purposes

EXPRESSING FEELINGS ABOUT THE STORY

- How did the story make you feel? Tell what parts made you feel this way.
- Why do you think other students might or might not enjoy reading this story/book?
- Would you recommend this book to someone else? Why or why not?
- Would you read another book by this author? Why or why not?
- What was going through your mind as you read this story?
- What was your favorite part of this story? Why is that your favorite?
- Which character did you like best or least? Why?
- Did your feelings change as you read this story? How?

NOTICING THE AUTHOR'S CRAFT

- If the author of this book were in our classroom right now, what would you say to or ask that person?
- If you could change this book, how would you change it?
- Is anything in this book strange or weird? Why do you think the author put that in the story?
- Did the author write this book in a special way (for example, lots of visual images, flashbacks, told in the first person)? Do you think that made this a better story?
- Why do you think the author wrote this story?

(Graham and Spiegel, 1996)

the main character, Beetle. What was Beetle like? What were her fears and hopes and dreams? What did she want out of her life? Once the girls identified with Beetle's issues, Jeni asked the question again, "How are you similar to the character?" This time, the answers both in the discussion and in the second journal entries were far more interesting.

Brianna's journal entry

> 1. Have ever felt like Alyce]
>
> 2. Yes, I have felt like Beetle, because sometimes when someone is gone, I work on a project for them but when they come back, they get mad because I didn't do it right. In this book, Beetle, trys to deliver a baby when the Midwife, Jane, isn't there. But, Jane gets ~~furious~~ irate with Beetle because she ~~pressed every thing~~ did everything wrong.

Laura's journal entry

> Have you Ever felt like the Chractor in the Book?   Feb. 18, 1997
>
> No Because I am not like the girl and I new my name in the begging and I was never a orphan.
>
> I changed my mind yes I felt like the girl in the book. One time I was trying to make cookeis for my mom's birthday and the burnt so I threw them in the trash. Also I had to do a speech in front of 100 people at Church. I had to clean my room in 5 minutes and I could not get it.

The experience with *The Midwife's Apprentice* group led to a strategy lesson that focused on taking apart prompts for underlying meaning rather than surface understanding.

OBJECTIVE: To help students think more deeply about prompts rather than answering at a superficial level

MATERIALS: Individual photocopies of probes (See page 102.)

STEPS:

1. Have the students list some of the prompts they have used in groups lately.

2. Ask students to report on how various prompts affected the quality of the discussion: What worked, what didn't, and why? Note how different answers lead to more or less interesting responses. For example, when students asked, "Would you read another book by this author?" they often answered "yes" or "no" with little explanation of why they felt that way. Students who used that prompt were able to talk about how quickly the discussion fizzled. Note the need for follow-up questions to keep the discussion moving and interesting.

3. Share the photocopied list of probes with students. You might also want to make a large copy for the wall or create a chart. Encourage students to note how probes help them use prompts more effectively.

4. Follow up by having students refer to probes as they work on their pre-discussion journal entries. Encourage them to keep the list of probes in front of them during the discussion so they can use it in their literature circle. During the whole-group debriefing, have them report on how probes affected their discussion.

Prompts and Probes

Prompt: **Have you ever felt like this character?**

Probes: How does the character feel?

Have you ever felt like that?

What does/did the character want or hope or need?

How are your experiences the same or different?

Prompt: **Would you read another book by this author?**

Probes: What were your favorite parts?

What did those parts have in common?

Did you like the main character?

Did you care what happened to him or her?

Prompt: **What questions would you like to ask the author?**

Probes: What didn't you understand?

What parts seem strange to you?

What parts didn't you like?

Why do you think the author wrote it that way?

Prompt: **What was the author trying to tell you?**

Probes: What were some of the things the main characters did?

What happened to them?

What were the results of their actions?

Prompt: **Do you think the main character did the right thing?**

Probes: What things did he or she do? (Brainstorm a lot of them.)

What other options did he or she have?

What do you think the consequences would have been if he/she had done something else?

Probes that work with almost any prompt:

Why do you feel that way?

What examples from the book make you think that?

How does that connect to what we were talking about before?

NOTICING AND WONDERING

A teacher we know taught her first graders to notice and wonder early in the year. During circle time, she would muse about such things as nature—"I wonder why the grass is green"—and have her students, in turn, try to think of something they noticed and wondered about: Why does it rain? Why do people fight? What makes a light bulb give off light? While these young children had a little trouble at first, the teacher made everyone try to think of something and she accepted all answers. After several days of this kind of talk, the students developed the habit of looking for things they noticed and wondered about because they knew their teacher would ask. Once the teacher turned "noticing and wondering" on, it was difficult to turn it off. Her students began to ask questions of the world constantly. Learning moved from a teacher-led task to a personal quest by students for understanding.

This is a wonderful model for oral and written response to literature. By teaching students to notice and wonder, we can help them become more aware of the world and about the things they read. I wonder why this character chose to do that? I wonder what I might do in his or her place? I wonder why the author ended the book this way? As they begin to ask and then answer these questions in their journals, their writing and their discussions show more awareness and more complex comprehension.

OBJECTIVE: To get students to wonder actively about characteristics of a book

MATERIALS: Picture book that invites discussion, such as *Tar Beach* (Ringgold, Crown)

STEPS:

1. Introduce the lesson by saying something like: "Wondering is an important thing that we do when we read. We often wonder about why things happen or what will happen next. Wondering helps us remember and understand what we read, it helps us figure out where our comprehension breaks down, and think about what we read.

When I read a book, I do a lot of thinking about the book as I read. I often wonder about why the author chose to do things, or why the characters in the book acted as they did. I also wonder about why the author chose the setting, what the answers to unexplained events in the book might be, what will happen next, and so forth. I'm going to read this story to you. After I read each page, I will stop to share with you some of the things I am wondering about as I read. I also would love to have you share some of the things you wondered about."

2. Read the first page and think aloud what you're wondering: "Right here, I am wondering about whether the little girl in this story is day-dreaming or if she is asleep. I wonder what it means when she says a 'tar beach.' Do you think she means a beach with tar . . . like something polluted? They are on the top of the building. I wonder if they are scared. I wonder if they go there often. Maybe in the summer it is fun to play up there.

    I also wonder why the author wrote this book about the city. Did she live there as a little girl or does she live there now? Maybe she knows lots of kids who live in the city. I wonder why the author made these pictures look like a quilt. I wonder if that will come into the story later."

3. Read the next few pages, continuing to reflect, while gradually giving over the questioning to the students.

4. Continue until children have all had several opportunities to share what they are wondering.

5. Follow up by having children practice noticing and wondering as they write journal entries. Encourage them to wonder as they listen to their classmates respond in groups.

During the whole-class reflection time, have them report on how wondering affected the discussion.

ASKING FOLLOW-UP QUESTIONS

As Jeni listened in on discussions, she began to notice that one of the things that keeps discussions going is students asking follow-up questions of each other. Follow-up questions allow students to clarify or explain or defend their thoughts. They include things such as, "Why do you think that?" "But what about this evidence?" or "Can you talk some more about why you think that?" When a student reads a journal entry and no one asks questions, the topic often fades. The ability to ask questions of what a person has said is basic to creating independence in discussion groups and learning, because it keeps the discussion moving and allows students to extend each other's thinking.

Jeni finds that when a student makes a comment, too often no one responds. The next speaker simply makes his or her own, unrelated remark. We feel that discussion can be greatly enhanced and thinking deepened if the students put more effort into listening to each other's remarks and asking follow-up questions.

OBJECTIVE: To encourage students to ask clarification and follow-up questions to enhance discussion and writing

MATERIALS: Picture book to provide material for discussion, such as *Working Cotton* (Williams, Harcourt, Brace, Jovanovich)

STEPS:

1. Explain to students that asking questions is important to keeping conversation moving. It helps group members who might have nothing to say—or who do, but need a hand finding the words.

2. Tell them that for this activity, they are the teachers. Their job is to do what the teacher always does—ask questions to help the reader think about what she read.

3. Read the picture book aloud.

4. Encourage students to ask you for your responses to the book. As the students ask questions, stop occasionally to draw more probing questions from students and to make them aware of their questioning behaviors. For example, Jeni might ask a questioner to tell her why he or she thought the question was good or bad. Or Jeni would inquire what might make a question better:

Jeni: I don't know if I would feel mad or sad. [pause] What would be a question to ask if I say that I don't know if I feel mad or sad? Karen?

Karen: Are you mad or sad?

Jeni: Think about how you could get me to understand how I would feel. What words could you use?

Karen: Well, how would you feel about being there?

Jeni: I am mad or sad and I am not sure which . . . I am going to tell you what I would say as a teacher, I would say, "What is the difference between being mad and being sad? When does something make you mad and when does something make you sad?"

A little later, Jeni continued reflecting aloud with Ryan, another student:

Ryan: Okay. It's my turn to ask the question. Ms. Day, would you read another book by this author?

Jeni: Yes. Absolutely. [long pause] What is your next question, Ryan?

Ryan: Next question?

Jeni: There is another question that leads right out of what you just asked me. Let's think aloud. You asked me if I would read another book by this author and I said yes. Is our conversation over? [to the class] What should Ryan do?

Ryan: Oh! I know! Why would you read another book by this author?

Jeni: Because I love the illustrations and because it made me feel strongly about young children working for a living.

The children quickly figured out that "yes" was not a very satisfying response. Jeni then helped the children think about how questions that elicited one-word answers need a follow-up question, such as Why? What makes you think that? or Could you explain a little more? to keep the discussion going.

This lesson helped students think about how questions help discussions flow and practice attaching follow-up questions to responses. Students became diligent in asking follow-up questions, and discussion flourished as a result. This behavior transferred to students' writing as well.

Strategy Lesson — ASKING OPEN-ENDED QUESTIONS

Once students become aware of asking each other questions they begin to notice that discussion flows very differently depending on the type of questions they ask. We want to focus their attention on the types of questions asked in discussions so that they can understand that different types of questions lead to different types of conversation. Closed questions, for example, have one right answer the asker is looking for: What is the capital of Virginia? Who is the main character? What did the main character do when she found out?, How was the problem solved?) while open questions have many possible answers. The prompts on the preceding pages are all examples of open questions. Students also benefit from classifying questions based on their purpose in conversation. When you ask an open question, you aren't sure what the person will answer. In real conversation we almost always ask open questions: Did you like the book? What do you want to do later? What did you do when you found out? We are asking because we really want to know. We are not testing our friends to find out what they know.

Other types of questions include asking for clarification, asking for reasons, challenging ideas, and confirming responses. It is often helpful to keep a chart of these on the wall for reference, which students can add to as they notice new types of questions.

Once students understand different types of questions, they begin noticing the questions they ask each other. They know to ask more open questions to create interesting writing and discussion.

OBJECTIVE: To help students determine how different types of questions affect discussion

MATERIALS: List of open and closed questions on the chalkboard or overhead, with definitions

STEPS:

1. Ask students to think about some of the questions they have used during their literature circles lately. Say something like: "I want to share some of the questions I have overheard some of you use in the last few weeks."

2. Show students your list of questions.

3. Encourage students to compare their questions to yours.

4. Have students report on how the different types of questions affected the quality of discussion. Say something like: "I noticed last week during literature circles that DeShawn asked, 'What do you think your little brother or sister would think about this book?' Do you think that might be an interesting question to discuss? Why or why not? In another group Sharon asked, 'Did you like the book?' Sharon, how did your group answer that question? Did it make the discussion interesting?" Sharon's group noted that it led to a lot of "yes" and "no" and not a lot of talk.

5. Define "open" and "closed" questions. Say something like: "I want to share with you one way I think about understanding different types of questions. Some questions we can think of as open and some as closed. Open questions encourage group members to talk rather than to give one-word answers because they require you to explain and because they ask for an opinion. Closed questions have just one right answer." Be sure to note that open questions make discussion more interesting.

6. Have students categorize questions into the two categories.

Questions, Categorized by Students

Closed Questions: Questions with one right answer

- What was the main character's name?

- Where did the main character live?

- When did this story take place?

- What happened first? What happened next?

Open Questions: Questions with many answers

- What do you suppose will happen next?

- Why do you think that happened?

- I don't understand what you mean. Can you give me an example?

- So do you mean . . . ?

- Does that remind you of the book we read earlier?

Final Thoughts

L isten in on any cafeteria conversation and you will see that students are able to carry on sophisticated discussions about siblings, sports teams, and the lunch menu. While discussing literature is not always easy, students are capable of doing it equally well. The strategies in this chapter will, hopefully, enable you to nudge your students' thinking, discussing, and writing about all things—but particularly, literature. In the next chapter, we offer assessment strategies to assist you in determining the success of literature circles.

CHAPTER 5

Assessing
Discussions

Before beginning this chapter, close the book and try to think about what you want your students to learn in literature circles. This is an important exercise for two reasons. First, we need to know where we are going in order to get there. (Jeni's mother still tells her, "If you aim for nothing, you're sure to hit it.") Second, students want to know what is expected of them and we need to be clear, for their sakes, about what our goals are so we can figure out how to know if we have reached them. This is where assessment by both the teacher and the students comes in.

In this chapter we explore the purposes and content of assessment, with specific ways to assess literature circles, including what to assess—what students talk about, how they interact in their groups, and the nature of their thinking about literature—and ideas on gathering information to answer these questions.

The Purposes of Assessment

There are three important reasons for assessing students' learning.

1. **To understand students' strengths and needs to determine the next instructional step.** Did the students seem to understand what we were trying to get across? If not, what is keeping them from understanding and what should they learn next or instead?

2. To communicate what is important to students. What the teacher chooses to evaluate is what the teacher thinks is important to remember. For example, students who have their writing graded primarily for spelling will tell you that to be a good writer you must know how to spell correctly. When students see their written ideas responded to, they begin to understand that writing is about communication and thinking through ideas.

3. To keep track of our own accomplishments as teachers. Were we successful at reaching all students? Did this method work or, more precisely, what did this method accomplish? If it didn't accomplish what we wanted, what might we do differently next time?

The Content of Assessment

We think of subjects such as biology, math, writing or history as having two parts, content and process. Content includes facts and concepts and theories. In science, for example, the content is the facts, the connections among facts, the relationships among ideas, while the process is the way scientists work, the scientific method of questioning, hypothesizing, testing and theorizing, and record keeping. Knowing the steps is not the only thinking involved; knowing how to apply them is also important.

It is the same for literature. We want students to know characters, what they are like and how they change, the purpose of symbolism, and that a plot with action can pull us in and keep us reading. However, we also want students to enjoy reading, to learn to read thoughtfully, to wonder about plot events, and to evaluate the author's work. We want students to think critically about what they read, rather than merely remember the book. We want students to be able to articulate what they don't like and give reasons. We want them to understand literary terms so they can explain more precisely what they do and don't like.

Both of these aspects of literature—content and process—are important in evaluating student learning in literature circles. Some teachers think that students should memorize and be quizzed on the content of the books—the names of the characters, the order of plot events, and the setting of the book. While these facts are important, this part of the content of literature is not relevant to learning to think about and enjoy literature. We enjoy the experience of reading good novels, but memorizing the names of the characters is entirely unrelated to our experience with the book. Learning the specifics of a book does not help children become better readers.

Assessing Literature Circles:
What and How

You can get a sense of what students understand about what they are learning by asking them, or by having a friend or colleague ask them. Jeni recently spent a lot of time observing in classrooms. She often asked students what literature discussions are about or what they think their teachers want them to learn. The answers were as varied as "to learn the book," "to fill out worksheets," "to get done quickly" or even "I don't know." Likewise they may say, "to talk," or "to share experiences." These very different answers tell a lot about what the teacher is communicating, often very subtly, to students about the purpose of what they are doing. When students don't understand the purpose of the activity, or

are more interested in finishing the activity than learning from it, we need to understand why.

If a student says that the purpose of literature circles is to learn the book, you may be focusing too much on memorizing facts from the book, and need to place more attention on responding to literature rather than learning it. (See Chapter 3.) If a student says the purpose is "to fill out worksheets," "to get done quickly," or "I don't know," you are probably not spending enough time brainstorming with students the purpose of literature circles and what happens during them. If students respond that the purpose is "to talk," or "to share experiences," they may be sharing responses but those responses may not be grounded in the text.

Data Collecting, Record Keeping, and Interpreting Results

Assessment comes in many forms, from formal tests to observation to portfolios to self-assessment. However, for all forms, it's important to collect data, keep records, and interpret the results to make informed decisions.

Data is the information we gather: Who has read which books, how long it took, what writing prompts students use or prefer, what kinds of responses they are giving.

Gathering data and keeping records of it is, in some ways, the easy part of assessment. The real challenge is interpretation—using records to gain a sense of how each student is developing. But interpretation is critical. It's why we gather data and keep records in the first place. It's where real teacher expertise comes in, forming a mental picture of what students can do, how they are understanding instruction, and what they might work on next.

The rest of this chapter is divided into three sections. The first explains how to gather evidence of students' progress in literature circles. The next section covers record keeping. We propose various ways of keeping track of the evidence of students' progress, such as checklists, logs, and interviews. The final section focuses on helping students become involved in their own evaluation.

DATA COLLECTING

What do we want students to learn from literature circles? Jeni developed a series of questions that she used as she observed and listened in. These questions helped her focus on particular areas. See Appendix B for a reproducible checklist of these questions. They can then be used to help you prepare for and observe discussions.

Do Students Understand the Purpose of Discussion? Our students don't always know exactly what to talk about in literature circles, even when we feel we have explained this quite clearly. Discussion is often a new idea for students, different from what they are used to doing in school. The rubric below can help you gauge their general understanding of discussion.

RUBRIC
Do Students Understand the Purpose of Discussion?

◆ Do students know what topics make for a good discussion? Do they have trouble beginning a discussion or shifting topics? ("What do we talk about?")

◆ Do they articulate what confuses them? ("I didn't understand why the character chose to return home.")

◆ Do students theorize about confusing sections of the text? ("I wonder if it means that she was sorry for what she had done?")

◆ Do they give evidence from the text for their opinions and evaluations? ("It says right here in the book that she was afraid.") What type of evidence do they give? Is it based on their own experiences of the text or something else? ("I would never do that if that happened to me.")

◆ Can students talk about who else might like the book? ("My little sister would like this book better than I did.")

◆ Do they try to understand the book from different perspectives, such as the author's, the main character's, or a classmate's? ("I think the author was making a point about how tough life was back then." "I don't like that the main character joined a gang, but I guess he felt he had to.")

MODELING GOOD QUESTIONS AND COMMENTS

Jeni thinks a great deal about what she says to her students and what it would sound like if the students said the same thing back to her. Modeling gives her a way to take apart a process and make it explicit to students. It gives her the opportunity to say the kinds of things she wants her students to say. And it's important for successful literature circles. If we model the kind of comments we want students to make, they will make them.

OBJECTIVE: To model for students the kinds of things we want them to say in literature circles

MATERIALS: A picture book or a chapter book

STEPS:

1. Remind students of the types of things they have listed that people talk about in literature circles. (See Chapter 2.)

2. Read the selection aloud.

3. Model comments about the text such as, "I didn't understand the part about . . ." and "I think the author was trying to say . . . ." See the rubric on page 115 for others.

4. Encourage students to make similar comments. Respond to them in the same way you would like students to respond to one another. "That's an interesting point," "I hadn't thought of it that way before," and "What Kelly said made me think of something interesting . . .." Before you say anything, think about how it would sound coming from one student to another or to you. Let that be the meter to judge the kinds of statements you model for students.

5. Later, during literature circles, listen to what students talk about and see if you notice changes in their discussion habits that reflect your modeling.

Are Students Interacting Well During Discussions? Helping students work together in groups is one of the most difficult and rewarding parts of literature circles. They need to be able to work together and respect each other. One way we accomplish this is by arranging the group so that each student is with at least one friend and not with someone he or she has a problem with. The following rubric helps us determine if the students can maintain their discussions with their classmates.

RUBRIC
Are Students Interacting Well During Discussions?

◆ Do students respond to each other's ideas? What are their responses like? Do they agree or disagree with each other's ideas? ("I agree that she was selfish, but I think she had reasons for being a brat. It wasn't her fault.")

◆ Are they willing to disagree? How do they go about disagreeing if they do? ("I don't think that's right. I think she had a good reason for being mean to her sister.")

◆ Are students willing to share tentative ideas, things they haven't thought through completely? ("I've been wondering if that wasn't because things were different then . . . well not different completely, but . . . do you know what I mean?")

◆ Do they ask questions of others? What types of questions do they ask? ("Did you like the book, Ryan? What do you think the character should have done?")

◆ How does student participation change when group configuration changes?

◆ If any of the items on this rubric are problems for your students, use the strategy lesson above "Modeling Good Questions and Comments," using this rubric as a guide. Again, model, and listen for, the kinds of things you want students to say.

What Is the Nature of Students' Thinking? Good discussion develops students' critical-thinking skills. Many students, however, are hesitant to question things in print or those in authority. The questions below will show how well students are able to think about what they read, form opinions, and learn from text.

RUBRIC
What Is the Nature of Students' Thinking?

- Are students willing to reconsider ideas in light of new evidence? What do students do when presented with conflicting evidence? ("That's a good point . . . I forgot that she had made the promise to her friend.")

- Do they actively theorize about the world or are they dependent on others to tell them the right answers ? ("Well, it might be that." as opposed to "I don't know. What do you think?")

- Are students willing or hesitant to disagree with sources of authority? ("I don't care if the books says . . ." as opposed to "Well, the book says so . . . so it must be true.")

- Do they see others as sources of expertise on which to draw? ("Let's ask Drew. He knows a lot about baseball.")

- When students give reasons for their opinions, are those reasons internal ("That doesn't fit my experience") or are they external, depending on outside authorities, including their parents, peers, friends, the book, or other adults? ("My teacher last year said . . ..")

- Do they see complexity in answers or do they just view them as right or wrong? ("I wonder if she was mean because of all the times people let her down," as opposed to "She was mean and that's all that matters.")

- Do students look for multiple explanations or does one suffice? ("He joined the army for excitement . . . or maybe he felt he had to join the army to help his sister . . . or maybe he wanted to get out of his terrible home situation.")

HELPING STUDENTS TO THINK CRITICALLY ABOUT TEXT

OBJECTIVE: To help students develop and accept multiple interpertations of a text

MATERIALS: A picture book that invites many interpretations, such as *The Giving Tree* by Shel Silverstein (HarperCollins), a story about a tree who loves a boy so much that she continues to give him everything she has: fruit, branches, and finally herself, leaving him only a stump, upon which he sits as an old man. While this story can be seen as a tale of unselfish love, it can also be seen as a story of an unhealthy relationship, in which one person gives and the other only takes, until the giver is destroyed.

STEPS:

1. Read the picture book aloud. Allow children to express their initial reactions to the story, by asking, "What did you think?" and "What do you think the author is trying to tell you?"

2. Encourage students to note alternate interpretations. If they don't, share your own, for example, "I don't necessarily think it's healthy for one person to always give in a relationship. I think the boy was selfish and unkind, and the tree shouldn't have been so generous." Or if the children note that interpretation, point out how important sacrifice is in loving someone. By focusing on the controversy, children begin to see that there is more than one way to interpret a book. They also learn that it is okay and valuable to have different opinions.

3. As the children provide more interpretations of the text, summarize controversies that arise (for example, "So Wanda thinks that the tree was showing unselfish love while Harold thinks that the tree should not have given the boy these things"), extend their ideas (for example, "Have you considered . . ." "What about . . ."), and continue to model acceptance for widely varying interpretations.

Do Students Use the "Language of Literature" in Discussions? Do they use literary terms? Or do they talk about ideas that they don't have names for? For example, one group kept talking about how they "couldn't get into" the book. They related that they just didn't care about the characters, that the characters didn't seem real, and that they didn't really care what would happen next in the story. While these fifth graders didn't know words for ideas like character development and suspense, they were describing those very things. This was the perfect time for a strategy lesson on those aspects of literature.

RUBRIC

Do Students Use the "Language of Literature" in Discussions?

- ◆ What sorts of language do students use to describe an author's decisions?

- ◆ Do they use terms such as character, setting, tone, theme, foreshadowing, and so forth? Do they talk about concepts such as these without having a name for them?

- ◆ Do students notice the sound and feel of the book's language? Do they attend to things such as metaphor and simile and how devices like them help us enjoy a book? Do they use the right terms to identify these devices?

Strategy Lesson USING LITERARY LANGUAGE IN DISCUSSION

Being aware of elements of literature can heighten students' awareness of what the author is doing. Just as awareness of line, shape, and color help us look more thoughtfully at artwork, awareness of setting, language, and symbolism can help us appreciate a book more.

OBJECTIVE: To help students become aware of how literary language can help them appreciate books more deeply and discuss them more precisely

MATERIALS: A picture book that vividly illustrates a literary concept—such as setting, character, or plot, for example, *Where the Wild Things Are* (Sendak, HarperCollins)

STEPS:

1. Introduce the concept. Say something like: "Today I want to share something that helps me appreciate books more. I notice that the setting of a book often reflects how a character feels or what he is going through. This happens in picture books and chapter books, but sometimes it's a little more obvious in picture books. I want to share with you this story, *Where the Wild Things Are*. But remember, this happens in chapter books as well."

2. Read the picture book, stopping occasionally to describe the setting and noting how it changes. Ask students for their thoughts, too. For *Where the Wild Things Are*, they might note that the pictures get bigger and messier as the book goes on, and then get smaller and neater again.

3. After reading, have the students speculate about what the changing setting might mean. Maybe the picture size relates to Max's imagination or his distance from his mother and order and rules, like you can't act wild.

4. Remind students to think about setting, or whatever literary idea you're addressing, when they write their first journal entry.

5. Later after literature circles, have students report during debriefing what literary devices they noticed in their books.

Great Picture Books for the "Language of Literature" Lesson

Rising Action, Conflict: Just about any good story works for this concept. Try Paterson's *The King's Equal* (HarperCollins), a lovely story about an arrogant prince and the woman who helps him.

Character Development: *Just a Dream* (Van Allsburg, Houghton Mifflin) is the tale of a boy who is unconcerned about the environment, until he travels to the future in a dream and sees the impact of his actions.

Theme: *The Wretched Stone* (Houghton Mifflin) is another book by Chris Van Allsburg containing "a big idea."

Setting: *Hey, Al* (Yorinks, Farrar, Strauss and Giroux), like Sendak's *Where the Wild Things Are*, has a setting that changes along with the characters.

Tone and Mood: Compare light and happy stories to mysterious and serious ones, such as *Working Cotton* (Williams, Harcourt, Brace, Jovanovich) and *Hey, Al.*

Foreshadowing: *The Lorax* (Geisel, Random House) is a Dr. Seuss story that begins with a picture suggesting what will happen later in the story.

Simile and Metaphor: Poetry is always good for teaching these concepts.

Rhyme: *I Can't Said the Ant* (Cameron, Putnam) is a fun story with wonderful rhyme.

Alliteration: Try alphabet books with alliterative statements for each letter, such as Graeme Base's *Animalia* (Scholastic).

These are only a few of the questions you might ask while observing literature circles. Students have different needs, abilities, and prior experiences. Teachers have different goals. Like prompts, using someone else's list may cause you to overlook interesting things that your own students are doing. So we encourage you to use our questions only as a starting point, and then form your own and start theorizing about what your students are thinking based on the kinds of things they say.

RECORD KEEPING

Having a system for keeping records helps you remain organized and makes data easier to interpret. Jeni uses a number of tools for keeping records on many aspects of her students' literacy growth and participation in literature circles. See the chart below.

Here are several of the forms Jeni developed and her reflections on them. For blank forms, see the appendices.

Assessment Goal	Assessment Tools
Keeping track of comprehension, reading levels, and journal quality	◆ Individual Reading/Book Logs (Appendix C) ◆ Student Journals ◆ Student Conferences (Appendix D)
Keeping track of the reading accomplished and prompts selected	◆ Class Log (Appendix E) ◆ Group Meeting Log (Appendix G)
Keeping track of the level and content of discussion	◆ Teacher Observation: Listening to live or recorded discussions, with a rubric ◆ Student Journals ◆ Teacher Daily Log (Appendix F)
Keeping track of students' self-assessments	◆ Spoken and Written Student Comments ◆ Group Meeting Log (Appendix G)

Individual Reading/Book Log

Student Name __Caryll__

Title	Author	Date began	Date finished
Bridge to Terebithia	Patterson	1/30	2/6
Cracker Jackson	Byars	or 1/30 2/6/97	2/20/97
Pin balls	Byars	2/28	3/4
Hey Al		3/21	3/21
Holes	Spinelli	3/28	—

INDIVIDUAL/READING BOOK LOGS

Individual logs are invaluable for providing a quick look at what children have read and how long they are taking to read. Stapling this to the inside of student response journals makes the journal entries easier to follow.

CLASS LOGS

Like book logs, class logs provide a quick look at each group's daily progress. During the writing time, while groups are finishing their discussions and returning to their seats, one student from each group tells Jeni what the group has agreed to read and write about for the following session. Jeni records the information in the log and uses it to keep the groups accountable.

	Date				
Student Groups	2/6/97	2/13/97	2/20	2/28	3/7
Group 1 Tanya Caryll Brianna Kate Kelly	Cracker Jackson– Ch 5-8 How are you like main ch?	Cracker Jackson– finish Choose new bk Would you rec. bc to another grp	Pinballs Ch 1-2 How does this comp to Crack Jackson?	Pinballs Ch 3-8 Would you do what Cracker did?	
Group 2 Drew AJ. Evan Ryan	Midwifes App. finish What Q's would you ask author?	Pinballs Ch 1-4 What does story remind you of?	Pinballs Ch 5-6 What is the most important thing that has happened	Pinballs finish Why did the author write this story?	
Group 3 Cale Laura Adele Brad	Bridge to Terebithia pp 1-55 How would you change this book if you could	Br. to T pp56-85 Are you more like Jess or Leslie?	Br to T finish What was the author trying to tell you	Just a Dream Ch Van A What Qs would you ask author?	
Group 4 Lucy Annie Katie Laura	Shiloh Ch. 1-3 What questns do you have so far for the author	Shiloh Ch 4-6 Would you recommend this book to someoneelse	Shiloh finish Did this book deserve to win Newbery Award?	Hey, Al What was the author trying to tell you?	
Group 5					

Group Meeting Log – [Completed after each discussion by group together or individuals   Date 2/13/97

Group members present _Drew, AJ, Ryan, Evan_

Group members absent _none_

Did everyone read the chapters and prepare a journal entry? _yes_

Book and Chapters read for today _Pincalls Ch 1-4_

Prompt(s) _What did the story remind you of?_

How did your group feel about this prompt?

(use it again)   don't like it   use it often

Topics discussed _What like to break egs, live in a faster home, how terrible it would be to have bad parents_

Good things that happened today.

Everyone was prepared

Everyone got into the discussion

Everyone liked the book

Were their any problems today?

_Students aren't asking questions and what do we do if some students get up and ___?_

How did your group go today? Was this better/worse than other groups in which you have participated?

_This was a great group – the ___ very exciting_

GROUP MEETING LOG

This form requires group members to collaborate in gathering information on what they are doing and encourages them to reflect after each meeting.

TEACHER DAILY LOG

This sheet helps focus your observations as you move from group to group during the block. It's designed to help you get to each group, write about specific events, and reflect on those events. The sheet can then be used to track students' growth and plan future strategy lessons.

Date 2/13/97	Observations	Reflections, Questions
Mini Lesson	Asking Teacher Qs – Working Cotton	This was great. I should let other students do this as well –
Group 1 Tanya Kelly Caryn Brianna Kate	Group is really focused with Tanya absent. Lots of neat topics	Should I move Tanya – I still feel this is the best grp for her –
Group 2 Drew AJ Evan Ryan	Drew asks questions of everyone – almost too many	Questioning seems forced – disappointg
Group 3 Cale Laura Adele Brad	Got to grp at end – and they finished early	Need to ask specifically how questioning went with this grp.
Group 4 Lucy Katie Annie Laura	Questions unrelated to discussion – More like drilling ea. other. Lucy is so good at	Need to capitalize on Lucy's ability to pull students in – maybe move to be w/ Tanya?
Group 5	helping other ss!	
Whole Class Discussion	Talked about whether asking Qs helped grps discuss – Students reported trying	Is forced question asking just a step toward getting it?

STUDENT SELF-ASSESSMENT

Self-assessment leads students toward becoming independent learners by helping them become aware of their own growth. As a result, they become able to participate in and plan their own learning.

Self-assessment is particularly important for literature circles for four reasons:

1. The nature of student-led discussion requires students to be independent, something they do not learn if the teacher is the only one evaluating their progress.

2. When students are responsible for their own assessment, they become more invested in their groups and the method of assessment.

3. One teacher can't possibly observe everything that happens in group discussions. And even if she could, would she want to? We find that a teacher's presence often changes the group dynamic, because the students are aware of being evaluated.

4. Paying attention to students' self-assessments provides information about students—such as their interests, motivation, and feelings about literature circles—that teachers cannot get in any other way. There is a vast difference between a student who says, "I did okay" and the student who says, "I think I am getting better at asking follow-up questions, but I still am quick to accept my first interpretation without trying to see how others might interpret the book."

What do you do well in literature circle discussions?

I get along with everyone (we all were into the conversation) I ask people what they are thinking I remind people during the week to finish reading and writing.

What problems does your group have?

We need a plan for who talks when we had lots of problems with interrupting Too loud - hard to hear

How has your participation in literature circles changed over the last __4__ weeks

I still talk too much but I am getting better at asking questions

What is one thing you would you like to get better at in literature circles?

Ask questions from everyone Ask good questions

We used three methods to help students think about their own progress:

- written accounts of their experiences
- class discussions of their experiences
- rubrics which the students helped to develop

WRITTEN ACCOUNTS

Having students keep written records of their experiences encourages them to reflect on their own behaviors within the group. Through writing, they begin to understand the connection between their own efforts and their enjoyment and success in discussions. Students also can examine their own growth over the year, which is far more useful than comparing themselves with other students.

CLASS DISCUSSIONS

Students reflect on how literature circles went during our whole-group discussions. We ask questions such as "What's working?" and "What needs work?" This activity accomplishes three things: Students realize that they often experience similar problems and can brainstorm solutions together. Students practice using the language of assessment by articulating what has gone well and what is still frustrating them. For example, "I still talk too much, but I am getting better at asking questions and waiting." Or "I still don't like to talk a lot, but I read my journal entry every week in group and am trying to write longer entries so I share more." Finally, it gives Jeni the opportunity to model a specific response about mistakes and problems, which helps students understand that mistakes happen to everyone and that we can choose to learn from them.

Here is a transcript of a discussion Jeni led where children talked about some of the problems they were having:

Jeni: I want to do some brainstorming now about some of the things that have gone well with our discussions and some of the problems we have had. I do want to ask one favor. When we talk about problems, we are not looking to place blame, but to consider how to get better. For example, instead of saying we were giggly, we should say that we need to be more serious. Do you understand what I am saying? So what do you think?

Amber: Should we change our topic to suggestions instead of problems?

Jeni: That's a good idea. Lets change it from problems to needs. So what do you think?

Frank: We were quiet and got along.

Sue: We all got a chance to talk.

Bradley: We all had like different opinions, like what we thought about the book was different, and so it was good for us to explain to each other.

John: We all got really into the conversation.

Liz: Our group had lots of different things they thought, but we were nice about our different thoughts.

Jeni: It sounds like your group was able to disagree agreeably, like on our list of guidelines. How about problems? Did anyone have problems?

Sue: It was kind of loud today?

Felix: Everyone was talking at once.

Jeni: That seems almost like two things that we could do, have smaller groups and find ways to help students listen to each other.

Amy: Yes, maybe smaller groups would help.

Pat: Our group didn't ask each other questions. We just read our journals and that was it. Nobody had any disagreements about the book.

Jeni: That's interesting. Do you have any idea why?

Pat: Well we all agreed, and we didn't have many different opinions.

Jeni: Several of you have mentioned that having different opinions is one of the things that makes groups good. Is that anyone else's experience?

[Several students agree.]

Jeni: Did anyone have a group that was too quiet? [silence] No? That's interesting. I want to go back to something someone said earlier, that people in their group didn't seem to be listening to each other. Can any of you think of a time when you knew someone wasn't listening to you? What does that feel like?

[Several students respond with stories of how their parents or friends didn't listen to something they said.]

Jeni: That can be frustrating. Think about that this week: How do you know when someone is listening to you? What kinds of things do they do? Thanks for helping us think through this.

Notice how Jeni frequently turns the discussion back to the students by asking for their opinions and to take apart what is happening (for example, when she asks, "Do you have any idea why the group didn't have any disagreements?" and "How can you tell when someone is really listening to you?" after asking them to think about what it feels like when people don't listen to you). She is learning with the students by working with them to determine what is going on in a whole-class discussion.

RUBRICS

Finally, by creating rubrics, students become aware of the goals of literature circles and when they understand their goals they are far more likely to accomplish them and think intelligently about them. By keeping track of topics that come up in student writing and whole-class discussions, you can help your students develop their own rubric.

Here is an example of a student-created rubric based on the discussion above. During this discussion, the students considered what real listening looks like. Once they understood that ignoring one another was a problem, Jeni led them to consider very specific ways to avoid that kind of conduct. Together, they crafted a list of more sensitive behaviors. With guidance from Jeni, that list was then changed to questions that students could ask themselves:

Checklist for Listening in Literature Circles

In today's literature circle I . . .	Not at all	One time	2-3 times
Faced the person who was speaking.			
Looked him or her in the eye.			
Nodded or somehow showed I heard him or her.			
Asked questions about what classmates said.			
Repeated parts I was not sure about.			
Asked classmates to repeat or re-explain parts that confused me.			
Smiled in a friendly way.			

Rubrics are especially helpful to use whenever you and your students begin to feel frustration with the progress being made in literature circles. They are also helpful at the beginning and ending of the marking period, when you and your students are reflecting on progress.

Final Thoughts

Assessment guides instruction. When we examine what our students are learning, we can tailor our instruction and solve specific problems that arise. Outside resources, such as books and workshops, can help but every class and every teacher is different, and, ultimately, there are no absolute answers for every situation. We can move forward only by assessing our own students and classroom practices carefully.

In the next chapter, we share some of the challenges that arose with specific students and provide suggestions that have helped us encourage all students' participation.

CHAPTER 6

Meeting *Diverse* Needs

These days, all teachers are likely to see students with special learning needs in their classrooms. Jeni is no exception. We want her whole class to be successful in literature circles, regardless of challenges some students face.

In this chapter, we start by making the case that discussion is critical for *all* learners. We describe four students with diverse learning needs in Jeni's class, and their participation in literature circles from November to early June. Finally, we offer interventions to help learners like them overcome barriers and become successful.

Literature Circles and Diverse Learners:
What the Research Shows

Traditionally, instruction for second-language learners and special-education students has been provided outside of the regular education classroom, so the context in which these students learn can be dramatically different from those of their peers (Allington, 1991). These programs, with few exceptions, have focused on the sub-skills of reading and literal information contained in texts (Johnston and Allington, 1991; Kelly, Farnan, and Richardson, 1996; Martinez-

Roldan and Lopez-Robertson, 1999-2000). These types of programs have come under considerable criticism from both those the special-education and the second-language learning communities (Garcia, 1990; Martinez-Roldan and Lopez-Robertson, 1999-2000; McGill-Franzen and Allington, 1993). Allington (1991) suggests that this attempt to slow down instruction and make it more concrete actually denies special education students literacy opportunities. Certainly, this type of instruction provides little opportunity for students to move beyond literal interpretations of books and enter new realms of thinking.

While these programs present the fewest opportunities for exposure to conversations, second-language learners and students in special education may have the greatest need for them. Gee (1992) argues that it is critical for second-language learners to learn the conversational practices of the mainstream community. Conversations are often carried on in different manners at home and at school for these students, requiring greater exposure to mainstream conversations at school. Literature circles offer students this exposure to conversations, as well as opportunities to practice their new language and engage in complex thinking.

Less proficient or inexperienced readers are also in need of exposure to conversations about books. These readers often fail to take an active role in understanding books (Gerla, 1996; Many, 1996). They seem to have difficulty using their personal experiences to help understand the text (Gerla, 1996; Many, 1996). They often fail to make the inferences needed to make a book meaningful and are less willing to work through their confusion (Many, 1996). These difficulties present major stumbling blocks for many struggling readers. When placed in instructional contexts that focus on isolated reading skills, they have few opportunities to develop these strategies. Reading becomes a chore and something that they do at school. During literature circles, these students can see modeled the types of processes that they can use to make books meaningful (Many, 1996).

Few researchers have examined how students with diverse needs participate in literature circles. However, the available work is encouraging. It demonstrates that diverse learners can learn to participate in small-group discussions of books independently (Goatley, Brock, and Raphael, 1995; Goatley, 1996; Raphael, Brock and Wallace, 1997; Martinez-Roldan and Lopez-Robertson, 1999-2000). It also shows that these students can make progress within literature circles. Students have shown progress in their ability to use personal connections to come to a deeper understanding of the text (Gilles, 1990; Goatley, 1996; Goatley et al., 1995; Kelly et al. 1996; Martinez-Roldan and Lopez-Robertson, 1999-2000; Raphael et al., 1997), to move beyond literal interpretations of text (Goatley, 1996; Goatley et al., 1995), to get along with others (Goatley, 1996; Goatley et al., 1995), to accept and value others' opinions (Goatley 1996; Goatley et al., 1995), and to become engaged in books and enjoy reading (Gerla, 1996; Throne, 1992).

Literature circles appear to be an effective way to give all students opportunities to think beyond literal interpretations, ask and answer questions, hear multiple perspectives, make inferences, explore ideas, elaborate, and evaluate. Providing these opportunities is seldom easy, but is critical in helping students with difficulties or differences to become lifelong readers. In addition, students with diverse backgrounds bring many perspectives to the rest of the students in the class, enriching and broadening the experience for the entire class.

A Close Look
at Four Students

*I*n the following section, we describe four students from Jeni's class who participated in literature circles from November to early June. At the start of the year, Jeni prepares her students for literature circles with a series of whole-class discussions. As the students learn, they move from whole-class to small-group discussions, so the responsibility for carrying out literature circles gradually shifts from Jeni to the students. (See Chapter 1 for details.)

We configure literature circles in three ways, again, with an eye toward gradually shifting control from teacher to student:

Literature Circles Offer Children With Diverse Needs Opportunities to

- Learn about common conversation practices.

- Practice a new language and express personal opinions and experiences.

- Engage in complex thinking such as exploring, evaluating, and elaborating on ideas, and moving beyond literal interpretations of books.

- Take an active role in understanding books and develop strategies to increase reading comprehension.

- Accept and value others' opinions.

- Become engaged in books and enjoy reading.

We start by mixing groups in terms of gender, ability, and race. Jeni organizes them and selects the reading material for each one.

Next, Jeni creates single-gender groups, and the students select their own reading material.

Finally, for the remainder of the year, the students organize their groups and select their reading material. (See Chapter 2 for details.)

EDDY AND JUAN: ENGLISH-LANGUAGE LEARNERS

Several of Jeni's students were learning English as a second language. We focused on two, both Spanish speaking. Eddy was a gregarious student. His English was frequently difficult to understand, but he persisted in getting his message across. He had been in the United States for three years. As an ESL student, Eddy was exempt from standardized testing, but we knew by listening to him read and examining his writing that his skills were below grade level. In the classroom, Eddy sometimes made comments that seemed unrelated to the topic or were clearly inappropriate. He was often impulsive in his actions and words. Because of Jeni's concerns about him, Eddy was evaluated toward the end of the year by the special education team, in Spanish, and was found to have special learning needs.

Juan, on the other hand, was an easygoing student who had been in the United States for only one year. His English was still limited, but he was quickly making progress. He was popular in the classroom and had many friends. His reading and writing in English were also clearly below grade level. Eddy and Juan were good friends and frequently helped each other in the classroom. Juan was less outgoing than Eddy and often depended on Eddy to help him.

EDDY AND JUAN'S PARTICIPATION IN LITERATURE CIRCLES FROM NOVEMBER TO JUNE

Literature circles presented Eddy and Juan with many challenges. Neither had a good grasp of English, so reading the books or even listening and understanding the stories was difficult. Since neither had participated previously in this kind of instruction, they did not have a good idea of what the discussions were for or what the teacher expected from them.

Group One

TIMEFRAME: weeks 5–8, 4 meetings
GROUP DETAILS: teacher organized, mixed gender
READING MATERIAL: teacher selected

When the students were assigned to their first small groups, Jeni continued to read the stories aloud to Eddy and Juan so they had the opportunity to hear the story and discuss any misunderstandings. In their small group were three girls who were all good readers and responsible students. The girls tried, usually unsuccessfully, to involve Eddy and Juan in the discussion. The boys were frequently disruptive.

However, there were times when Juan and Eddy discussed the story seriously, usually when the girls asked them about their unique experiences in relation to the book. In the following example the group is again discussing *Baseball Saved Us* (Mochizuki, Lee & Low). Juan relates his own and the character's experience of coming to the United States and helps Kate understand this experience more fully.

> **Kate:** Juan how did you feel on your first day in America?
> **Juan:** Because the man is looking at the boy and the boy is look at the
> man and the boy is, I don't know, because the man is looking . . .
> **Kate:** Yeah, the guy in the tower is looking down. Well, is that how
> you felt because everyone was looking at you?
> **Juan:** Yeah.

Group Two

TIMEFRAME: weeks 9–16, 8 meetings
GROUP DETAILS: teacher organized, single gender
READING MATERIAL: student selected

In their next literature circle, Juan and Eddy participated with three other boys. Initially, this group seemed to have even more difficulty with Eddy and Juan than the previous group. Eddy continued to make comments that were off topic and disruptive to the discussion. Juan did not appear to be involved in the group at all.

The other boys asked Jeni to intervene, and she discussed the problems with the group. She wanted the group to take ownership for the problems and to find solutions. The group brainstormed possible solutions. Jeni knew from the previous group's experience that these two students could at times participate appropriately in discussions, so she wanted to increase the frequency of this occurring. She wanted to provide the group with a strategy to handle the disruptive behavior again: "If Eddy wants to join you, he can. If he wants to play, let him talk. Just don't pay any attention to him and just keep doing what you're supposed to be doing. If you pay attention and listen to him, he's just going keep talking about silly stuff. If he wants to be listened to, he needs to be serious."

However, the group's problems did not end with that advice. Choosing a book for the group to read caused great difficulty for Eddy, Juan, and other members. Eddy had difficulty agreeing on anything to read. In a whole class meeting, Eddy commented, "I just cannot read." Again, Jeni involved the whole group in trying to find solutions to their problem. After discussions with Jeni, the group decided that Eddy and Juan would skip the first novel. Instead they would begin reading the novel the group would discuss next. With Jeni's help, the group agreed to read *The Year of the Panda* (Schlein, HarperCollins) as their next novel. This would allow Juan and Eddy extra time to read, so they would not be concerned about keeping up with the group. Eddy and Juan read to each other aloud in the back of the classroom as the others were discussing the first novel. Jeni answered questions as they arose. The boys appeared engaged as they read. They seldom took their eyes off the book and talked to each other as they read. Both Eddy and Juan participated in the discussion of that book enthusiastically and appropriately.

These two interventions appeared to support Juan and Eddy sufficiently so that they could participate successfully. In addition, the book they read, *The Year of the Panda*, interested Eddy because it was on one of his favorite topics, animals. During the discussion he commented: "The book was very great to me. They need more characters like bear like . . . I love the book because the pandas, they are beautiful animals, they are like, I was . . . It's a boy, it's a Japanese boy, a Chinese boy, but he loves pandas. I said to the writer, I kill no panda because if I kill the panda, the panda not going to be anymore in the world."

With this statement, Eddy demonstrated that he could relate his own experiences with the main characters, could notice the craft of writing, and could understand the message the author was trying to convey.

Group Three

TIMEFRAME: weeks 17–23, 7 meetings
GROUP DETAILS: student organized, single gender
READING MATERIAL: student selected

Juan and Eddy were not in the same group at this stage. In this last group, Juan's participation dropped sharply. Members of his group accused him of not reading the book, which he vehemently denied. It appeared that Juan needed the support of reading the novel with Eddy or another student. Without this support, Juan's participation suffered.

Eddy continued to participate in his third group. He also showed improvements in his participation from the beginning of the year. He made comments on the book and made genuine attempts to understand what he read. He asked questions of his peers and responded to their questions. The following is an example of Eddy's participation in his final group. The boys discussed why the main character in *Nothing but the Truth* (Avi, Orchard Books) was not on the track team if he was such a good runner:

> **Jack:** And then when he goes and says he's a good runner . . .
> **David:** Then the next day he's off the team.
> **Jack:** So then people say he's not a good runner.
> **Eddy:** Is he good runner or bad? I don't know where he only stay in bed like that.
> **David:** He's supposed to be on a team but he didn't have enough good scores.
> **Eddy:** But homework. He didn't do no homework.
> **Jack:** Yeah, he didn't have good scores, so if you're not a good, if you don't study a lot . . .

WHAT WE LEARNED FROM EDDY AND JUAN

The Importance of Accessible Text One significant barrier to Eddy and Juan's participation was their difficulty in reading the books. Jeni provided many successful interventions which made the texts more accessible for them and other students. She read the stories aloud initially, for example. This allowed the students time to learn about discussion without the burden of reading independently. Having Juan and Eddy participate in fewer discussions enabled them to spend more time with texts, which bolstered their participation in the discussion. When Eddy read *The Year of the Panda*, we saw how providing books that matched student interests and experiences could make a huge difference in student participation.

We also became sensitive to behaviors that may signal a student's need for additional support. For example, when Juan was separated from Eddy, his participation dropped sharply. He withdrew after showing us that he could participate. This may have been a sign that he was unable to adequately access the text without Eddy's support.

The Importance of Grouping Grouping either facilitated or inhibited Eddy and Juan's participation in discussion, depending on the whole group's configuration. We found it difficult to predict which classmates would be supportive. We put them in a mix-gendered group initially because we thought the girls would provide direction and support for Eddy and Juan; however, this was not always the case. When the girls "babied" the two boys, or told them what to say, Eddy and Juan responded by being silly.

In addition to group configuration, we found that the way Jeni gave them directions was important. For example, when she told the other students to ignore inappropriate behavior, members felt they "owned" the problem, and Jeni provided a strategy to handle it. As Juan and Eddy began to interact more appropriately, the other students were then able to treat them as valued and contributing members of the group and their participation increased.

SHARICE: A RELUCTANT PARTICIPANT

Sharice was hesitant to talk during class. She never contributed to class discussions unless questioned directly and even then sometimes declined to participate with a shrug of her shoulders. She scored at the fifteenth percentile on a standardized test of reading and did not view herself as a good student.

SHARICE'S PARTICIPATION IN LITERATURE CIRCLES FROM NOVEMBER TO JUNE

Group One

TIMEFRAME: weeks 5–8, 4 meetings
GROUP DETAILS: teacher organized, mixed gender
READING MATERIAL: teacher selected

In her first group Sharice was with Tanya, one boy, and another girl. For all four sessions with this group, she seemed to have genuine difficulty saying anything. In an interview around this time she reported, "I just can't never think of nothing to say." Sharice made only two or three contributions to each discussion, usually toward the beginning of the meeting. Most often these contributions consisted of responding to questions.

Tanya tried to involve her in the discussion. However, these attempts were largely unsuccessful. In the following example, when discussing *Baseball Saved Us* (Mochizuki, Lee & Low), Tanya tried to tell Sharice what to say:

> **Tanya:** Ain't you talking, Sharice? I know what Sharice can say.
> Sharice, you can say . . .
> **Bradley:** Why don't you let Sharice say whatever she wants?
> **Tanya:** I know, Sharice. You can say, like, I would never want to feel
> that way because it makes me sad and stuff like that. But think
> about it. Don't you ever get nervous when you go up to make a
> presentation?
> **Sharice:** Yeah.

Tanya: Well, that's what you need to say.

Sharice: I wouldn't never want to feel that way because it makes me mad.

As with Eddy and Juan, directly telling Sharice what to say was not a useful strategy to increasing her participation. She generally repeated what Tanya had said, but then went silent again.

Sharice also had difficulty generating any kind of written response in her journal in the initial stages of literature circles. She responded in her journal only after the discussion. She wrote the following journal entry only after listening to the class discussion of Van Allsburg's *The Wretched Stone* (Houghton Mifflin):

> *I think the author was trying to tell us about the rock. I think the rock is bad because the rock wanted the people to just look at him and not learn anything.*

As she was exposed to the ideas and discussion of the group, her own ideas about what she was reading began to take shape and by the fourth (and last) session with this group, Sharice was generating ideas in her journal prior to discussion.

Group Two

TIMEFRAME: week 9–16, 8 meetings
GROUP DETAILS: teacher organized, single-gender
READING MATERIAL: student selected

In the second group, Sharice was with Tanya and three girls labeled academically gifted. Sharice's spontaneous participation in this group continued to be at a low level as in her first group, in spite of efforts by other group members to get her to talk. Kate, Annie, and Tanya often asked Sharice her opinion.

Now that Sharice was consistently writing journal entries she participated in each session by reading her journal. However, Sharice often could not or would not respond to questions by other group members that asked her to explain her responses. For example, several times she pronounced a book boring in response to the prompt "Did you like the book?" But when queried, she could not explain why. In fact, she seemed unsettled by these questions, declaring in jest at the last session with this group, "Y'all ask me one more question, I am going to kill myself." Sharice would refer back to what she had written but seemed unable to elaborate on these prepared responses.

Sharice also discussed procedural details such as which chapters to read and which books to read. As she grew more comfortable with the group, she was able to provide some spontaneous contributions to the discussion. These comments did not demonstrate a deep understanding of the book but they did show an emerging ability to contribution to the discussion.

Group Three

TIMEFRAME: weeks 17–23, 7 meetings
GROUP DETAILS: teacher organized, single gender
READING MATERIAL: student selected

This final group, organized by the students themselves, included Sharice, Tanya, one boy, and another girl, students with whom Sharice socialized in and out of school, and she was comfortable with them. Therefore, Sharice was more vocal than she had been in either of the other two groups, especially about procedural and social matters.

Sharice contributed more spontaneously and frequently to the discussions, although her contributions were usually perfunctory. For example, in at least two of the seven sessions, she corrected group members' pronunciation. Most of her other comments were procedural, although at least once she showed the ability to relate to a character, while discussing *The Noonday Friends* (Stolz, HarperCollins):

> **Sharice:** I think . . . because her dad doesn't have a job and she can not see her friends.
> **Theresa:** I don't understand that real good.
> **Sharice:** But my mom . . .
> **Theresa:** If my mom didn't have a job and she wouldn't let me be with my friends right, I don't know what I would do.
> **Sharice:** I know. I'd run; I'd fly away.

In group three, Tanya came into her own as a leader. In the first session of this group, Tanya was just feeling out her leadership role, and Sharice was a major player in this session. But as Tanya became more assertive, Sharice made fewer substantive contributions, although she still was more involved than in either of the other two groups.

Sharice was clearly more at ease in group three than in the earlier groups. However, there was a trade-off for this level of comfort. Sharice was sometimes disruptive to the discussions. She had unrelated side conversations with others in the group, did not attend to the conversation at times, and made distracting remarks. At one point, when Sharice was being disruptive, Tanya said to her "We're getting a grade on this, Sharice, and if I fail, I'm going to blame you."

WHAT WE LEARNED FROM SHARICE

The Importance of Grouping As with Juan and Eddy, group membership was a critical factor for Sharice. However, anticipating how the group composition would affect her was difficult. We placed Tanya in Sharice's group as a support; however Tanya was not always as helpful as we hoped she would be. While Tanya made genuine attempts to prompt Sharice to talk more, she was often unsuccessful.

Telling these students what to say was not an effective strategy for increasing participation. Tanya often overwhelmed Sharice, and Sharice often found it easier just to remain silent. In hindsight, placing these two students in different groups for at least one of the cycles would have been beneficial.

We also found that length of time in a group also had some effect on participation. In group two, Sharice made spontaneous comments only after the first five sessions. While her participation remained limited, there was a shift in the type of participation as she came to trust the others in the group.

Composing groups was tricky because we had to determine whether the interaction among *all* students was working for *each* student. We found that observing and talking to students, and changing group membership as necessary, was helpful.

The Importance of Journals A second understanding we gained was the importance of journal writing in conjunction with discussion, particularly for shy or reticent students. Initially, journal writing assisted Sharice in generating something to say during group discussions. Raphael and her colleagues (1997) hypothesized that allowing children to write in a journal allows students "private space" to compose their thoughts, thereby encouraging response. For Sharice, it also provided time to formulate a response. When we interviewed her we were struck by the length of time she sometimes took to formulate a response to our questions. This time would be less available to her in peer discussions because of the fast pace.

Once Sharice began to respond in her journal before coming to literature circles, she had something to say. She usually said it early, reading from her journal, and then made few contributions after that, except for procedural matters. While the journal gave Sharice the confidence to join in the discussion at least once each session, she was unable to elaborate on what she had prepared. Sharice might have benefited from some individual coaching in this area. We describe how we might have carried this out in the second section of this chapter.

TANYA: AN EMERGING LEADER

Tanya was reading in the low-average range, according to standardized test results. She was outgoing and sometimes participated with enthusiasm in classroom activities. She often offered insightful comments and suggestions. However, at other times Tanya's behavior was problematic. She often had to be reminded not to bother other students. She was impulsive, easily frustrated, and frequently lashed out verbally. Sometimes she withdrew, sucked her thumb, and pouted.

TANYA'S PARTICIPATION IN LITERATURE CIRCLES FROM NOVEMBER TO JUNE

Group One
TIMEFRAME: week 5–8, 4 meetings
GROUP DETAILS: teacher selected, mixed gender
READING MATERIALS: teacher selected stories

For all four sessions of the first group, either Jeni read a story to the class or she assigned a common short story from *Cricket* magazine, which Tanya could read easily. Tanya participated fully in these sessions and often took a leadership role. Here she could be actively involved without risking making comments in the whole class. She initiated topics, listened to others, and expanded on their comments. Tanya was engaged, enthusiastic about sharing her ideas, and interested in others' opinions. In the following example, she tries hard to get the group to discuss the ideas in *Baseball Saved Us* after they have presented their journal entries:

> **Carolyn:** I'll go. I don't think I have ever felt like that and so I am very lucky sometimes. If there's someone in my class with a weird name or someone very strange, I might laugh at them, but as the year goes on I find they're not so weird at all, just like in the story.
>
> **Sharice:** I don't have one [a journal entry].
>
> **Tanya:** Well, I feel like him in situations where I do presentations and I think when I go up, there are people that make fun of my presentations and it makes me mad because I've been rehearsing.
>
> **Bradley** (*to group*): Say something . . .
>
> **Tanya:** Don't you feel like that? [pause] I never want to feel that way.
>
> **Sharice:** I never want to feel that way.
>
> **Carolyn:** What do we do now?
>
> **Tanya:** The book was kind of boring.

Group Two

TIMEFRAME: week 9–16, 8 meetings
GROUP DETAILS: teacher organized, single gender
READING MATERIALS: student selected

Tanya was with Sharice, plus three other girls who were all designated as academically gifted. For the first two sessions of the second group, Tanya participated fully and enthusiastically in the discussions about the short stories Jeni had assigned. However, as soon as the group had to select their own reading material, Tanya's behavior changed. At times, she refused to discuss the book, stalking off from her group. She frequently turned her back on the group or rolled on the floor sucking her thumb. She teased others in the groups and was sarcastic in her responses. She displayed anger toward her group, for example, by slamming her book on her desk. Jeni tried several times to address Tanya's behavior. Jeni talked to her and sometimes removed her from the group for short periods of time. Each time the group selected a book that was hard for Tanya, her behavior deteriorated. When she behaved in this way the rest of the group ignored her.

Even when her behavior improved, it generally took more than one session of benign behavior for the others to stop ignoring her. Sometimes Tanya was ignored no matter what she said, even when her comments were insightful. For example, during this discussion of *The Pinballs* (Byars, HarperCollins):

> **Carolyn:** I kind of felt alone sometimes, just because, like my family
> would make decisions and they wouldn't, like, let me in on them,
> like with the cat's name.
>
> **Kate:** Well, that's different from Carly or Joey.
>
> **Tanya:** But they're not really family. They're like close friends.
> They're not really family, you know, by law, but . . .
>
> **Kate** (*interrupting*)**:** Sharice, would you like to go?

Group Three

TIMEFRAME: weeks 17–23, 7 meetings
GROUP DETAILS: student organized
READING MATERIAL: student selected

*I*n this group, Tanya was the clear leader. For most sessions, she selected the book and prompt, she initiated the discussion, and, if the others didn't immediately cooperate, she scolded them. As Sharice said, "She's the boss. Listen to her."

Tanya's responses were often quite sophisticated. For example, in discussing *The Noonday Friends*, she expressed impatience with the unemployed father in the book who prevents his daughter from playing with her friends. Tanya's solution was mature and simple: "If I was her, I would sit down and talk to my father and I

would like, well, what does me and my friend have to do with you not having a job right then?" She got to the heart of the book: "It's like friends that's very close, and then that friend stop the friendship, start breaking apart. That's when they have to work out. That's when it's really tough, sort of telling me about friendship." In just these two examples we learned that Tanya can read the book, put herself in a character's place, and identify theme.

WHAT WE LEARNED FROM TANYA

The Importance of Accessible Text Our experiences with Tanya illustrated the importance of ensuring that group members choose books that they can all read. Clearly, Tanya's ability, or her perception of her ability, to read the book heavily influenced her participation in the group. Most likely this behavior was unconscious, but whether intentional or not, it followed the maxim "If I sleep on the floor, I can't fall out of bed." In other words, Tanya's inappropriate behaviors prevented her from having to exhibit her lack of ability to read the book because she either did not or was not allowed to participate in the discussions. In retrospect, it may have been beneficial to all students if we had been more proactive in helping groups select books. Jeni did give book talks and specific instructions about choosing a book, which interested everyone in the group. But we did not spend enough time accommodating different reading levels.

Interventions
to Promote Success for All Students

Based on our observations, we pinpointed three major barriers to participation in literature circles:

- ◆ Students may have difficulty accessing the text.
- ◆ Group membership may not support each student's growth.
- ◆ Individual students may lack the skills necessary to participate.

These barriers can be lifted, however, through thoughtful and carefully timed teacher intervention. Later in this chapter we describe interventions for each of these three areas, but, first, we discuss the timing and extent of intervention more generally.

Determining the Timing
and Extent of Intervention

Deciding when and how to intervene is complicated and depends heavily on knowing your students and your own personal style. Examination of student behavior is the first step. We find that a change in a student's participation is a fairly good indicator of a problem. When Tanya was able to read the selected text, she participated enthusiastically in the discussion. When she could not read the book (or believed she could not) her behavior changed s uddenly. She pouted or lashed out angrily. When Juan was no longer paired with Eddy and did not have a buddy to read with, he became withdrawn.

The next step is to look for barriers to the student's participation. It's important to identify the problem so that the intervention can target that specific barrier. Examine the book, the group, and the student's skills to try and determine where the problem lies. Is the book too difficult? Is the grouping of students conducive to discussion? Does the student have the necessary skills and tools to discuss the book?

The last step is to choose the extent and form of intervention. Interventions can be at the whole-class, small-group, or individual level, and may take the form of quick strategy lessons or more intensive direct instruction. Problems occurring in several groups can be handled through whole-class discussions and strategy lessons while problems that seem idiosyncratic to one group or child can be handled through individual or small-group conferences. The more difficulty a student appears to have, the more direct your approach is likely to be. We suggest you tackle one problem at a time. Use a gradual approach in handling the problems.

The Timing and Extent of Intervention: Steps to Take

◆ Determine levels of participation. Be alert to sudden drops or changes in students' contributions.

◆ Determine what might be the barrier to participation (text difficulty, grouping issues, or lack of skills).

◆ Determine the level at which the problem is occurring (whole class, small group, or individual student) and the form of intervention required (strategy lessons, modeling, or direct instruction).

The discussion of interventions is organized around the three major barriers listed earlier.

Interventions

Ensuring Access to Text

- Read books aloud, have students partner read, or provide books on tape.

- Encourage repeated readings.

- Provide alternate texts.

- Require fewer discussion groups.

- Work on comprehension of content and structure, literary concepts, or vocabulary.

Forming Groups That Support Each Student's Growth

- Pair students who need support with those who can give support.

- Be cognizant of group dynamics and change membership as often as needed.

Coaching Students Who Are Struggling

- Determine the discussion skills that need to be taught.

- Engage the student in identifying the problem.

- Engage the student in solving the problem.

- Focus on what the student is doing right.

ENSURING ACCESS TO TEXT

Providing books that are accessible to all students may be one of the most daunting challenges teachers face. Students in a single classroom read at many different levels. Selecting a book that is both interesting and understandable to children at varied levels is difficult. But if a book is not accessible to a student, if she or he cannot read the book, that child will not be able to participate in any discussion of it.

Diverse learners may have difficulty accessing text for a variety of reasons. One of the primary reasons is difficulty decoding the text: The student can't read the words. However, this is not the only reason readers may have difficulty. Some students may have difficulty understanding the book's vocabulary. Students with learning difficulties may have difficulty remembering the characters and their actions and, therefore, may not be able to follow the flow of the plot. Those with language impairments may not recognize the structure of the text and may be unable to use that structure to help them understand the book. English language learners may be unfamiliar with some of the structures presented to them in books because stories from other cultures can be structured differently from traditional English-language stories. Students from other cultures may also have difficulty because books may describe experiences that are not familiar to them. There are several interventions you might consider to help make books more accessible to all students. Many of these interventions have been discussed earlier in the book, as their benefits can be helpful for all students in your class. (See Chapter 3.)

READ BOOKS ALOUD

Reading books aloud is one way to circumvent difficulties with decoding the words in the text. This will allow students to concentrate on the meaning in the text. However, this will not resolve the students' word-level difficulties with reading. These difficulties can not be ignored and should be addressed at another point in the students' program. For the teacher to read everything aloud would be extremely time consuming, but other ways of having the book read aloud are available, such as partner reading, books on tape, sending the book home for a relative to read, or computer programs such as *Write:OutLoud*, volume 3 (Johnston, 1999), which read material available on disk aloud.

ENCOURAGE REPEATED READINGS

Students may need to reread the book, chapter, or story several times before they can feel confident enough to discuss the book with their classmates. Allowing them the time to do this can be valuable. Repeated readings can take many forms. Students can read books in pairs and then independently, or a book can be read aloud and then independently. Variety will make the repeated readings more appealing to students. Rereading the whole book is also not always necessary. Sometimes rereading a particularly difficult section can be beneficial.

Retellings and reenactments of stories can also be used to enhance understanding. Many teachers of regular education students have found that acting out stories has been helpful to their students. Nielsen (1993) found that low achieving students benefited most when small-group activities included repeated retellings and reenactments of stories. Janet has also found acting out stories to be beneficial in her special education class for increasing students' understanding of the story. Students often enjoy this activity so much they ask to act out the story again and again!

PROVIDE ALTERNATE TEXTS

Alternate texts are sometimes available for students to read. Selected students read and discuss an abridged version of the book which the rest of their group is reading in its original version. While these students will not get all the nuances of the original version of the book, they will be able to participate with confidence because they have read the material. When using alternative texts, however, it is important that the students understand that there may be slight differences in the books they read.

For English-language learners, some books may be available in their primary language. This is especially true for Spanish speakers. A twist on this is to find a book written in a student's native language and provide the other students with an English translation. However, keep in mind that English-language learners need ample opportunities to read in English as well as their native language.

REQUIRE FEWER DISCUSSION GROUPS

Students who find it difficult to read quickly enough to keep up with the group may be allowed to participate in fewer literature circles. For example, these students may participate in discussions for every second novel. This allows the students extra time to read or reread. Jeni used this strategy when she noticed that Juan and Eddy's second group was having difficulty finding a book that all the boys could read. The extra time and the second reading of the novel allowed them to feel confident and increased their participation. This will not work, however, if the book is too far above the students' current level of comfort.

WORK ON COMPREHENSION OF CONTENT AND STRUCTURE, LITERARY CONCEPTS, OR VOCABULARY

Diverse students may have difficulty understanding text for several reasons. Students from other cultures may be unfamiliar with the structure of English-language texts or with the experiences described in the texts. Students with learning difficulties may be unable to recognize the structure of texts or the author's use of literary devices and may, as a result, have difficulty comprehending the text. Strategy lessons can help struggling students understand the language and structure of texts. See Chapter 3 for examples of these lessons.

Diverse learners may also have difficulty with the vocabulary used in the book. One strategy is to ask the student to identify which words are causing a problem. You can then discuss the meanings of those words with the student and have him or her reread the story.

Having students identify vocabulary they don't understand is helpful in at least three ways. It gives them, not the teacher, the opportunity to identify the words they don't understand. Your assumptions about which words are causing problems may not be accurate. This strategy also gives you an idea of how much difficulty a student is having. If the reader identifies many words, more than likely the book is too difficult, even with substantial intervention. The best course of action would be to choose a different story. Finally, it helps students begin to analyze and monitor their own comprehension. They start to ask themselves "What do I understand? What don't I understand? What additional information do I need? Why don't I understand this?" This task is often difficult for students struggling with reading and language, but guidance and practice in identifying the sources of their reading difficulties will pay off.

FORMING GROUPS THAT SUPPORT EACH STUDENT'S GROWTH

We have learned that grouping is an important factor for all our students. Students change in their level of participation depending on the group of students they are with. Tanya put it well: "Book clubs are fun. It just depends on the people you're with and the books that you read."

Pairing a struggling reader with a more successful reader is useful. The more successful reader can model appropriate strategies, suggest strategies for the strug-gling reader to use, provide occasional words, ask guiding questions, and generally be available to help out when the other student has difficulty.

However, group interactions are extremely complex and somewhat unpre-dictable. It is often difficult to predict who will actually be helpful to a struggling student. Sometimes it is not the top student in the class who is the most helpful. In spite of our best efforts, groups are formed that are not successful, or that, after a good start, become a problem. It is important to be alert to this and change the grouping as needed. In retrospect, we probably allowed the second round of groups to stay in place too long. Both Sharice and Tanya would have benefited from an earlier change in group membership.

In addition, pairing children for the purposes of support should never be a substitute for having students reading materials at the right level. Teachers must not use this strategy in ways that create learned helplessness. That is, a struggling reader should not be expected to read a book that is too hard, even if she or he is given a peer as a helper. A good rule of thumb is to remember that the more successful student can support the less successful student only if the struggling reader can almost be successful without help.

One final word about pairing students: Children occasionally need to be separated, not paired, but some just shouldn't be in the same group. You should find other opportunities for these students to learn to get along together. Literature circles are too important and too complex to use as arenas for improving social relationships.

COACHING STUDENTS WHO ARE STRUGGLING

Most students need time to learn how to respond to literature because they are trying out new ways of interacting and thinking, but some may have more difficulty than others. This is especially true for diverse learners. For example, students with special learning needs may need increased guidance in when and how to share during book club. If students are from different cultural backgrounds, they may have learned different ways of participating in discussion that are not consistent with your classroom practices. Students with learning differences may have difficul-ty sticking to the topic or may fail to seek clarification when they don't understand.

They may have difficulty gaining and maintaining the attention of the group or they may dominate the discussion, not relinquishing a turn to others. If whole-class strategy lessons or discussions, which are explored earlier in the book, or the suggestions provided in the chapter thus far have not resolved the problems for specific students, the difficulty may need to be addressed through more intensive individualized instruction (Goatley, 1996). Here is one possible approach:

DETERMINE THE DISCUSSION SKILLS TO BE TAUGHT

Once you note that a student is having difficulty, and that the difficulty is not related to book difficulty or grouping, determine what skills the student is having difficulty with during discussions. Is the student dominating discussion? Does she or he take turns when it is appropriate? Does she or he interrupt other students when they are talking? Are the student's comments relevant to the discussion? Does this learner ask for clarification? Does he or she ask for clarification too often? When and under what conditions does the student participate successfully? It is critical that the nature of the student's discussion skills be described as clearly as possible, especially for diverse learners, who may perform well under one set of conditions but not under another. For example, if Jeni had observed Juan only when he was paired with Eddy, she might have concluded that he was doing well in literature circles.

Diverse learners often have more than one area of difficulty or difference. Sharice was a struggling reader, so at times she was asked to read materials for discussion that were very difficult for her. She also was naturally reticent, a quality that made her a listener rather than a true participant in discussion. Tackle one area at a time.

ENGAGE THE STUDENT IN IDENTIFYING THE PROBLEM

Hold a conference with the student who is in need of individual instruction to discuss what he or she has noticed in the literature circles. One technique is to say something like "I have noticed that you interrupt the others when you try to take your turn in book clubs. The other students seem to get annoyed. Have you noticed this?" This statement has three parts: (1) an identification of the specific problem or issue, (2) a description of the consequences, and (3) an attempt to engage the student. This is important because students need to understand what it is they must change or learn, why and they must be actively involved in the process in order to make optimal progress.

The student may not have noticed any problem or consequences. This may be especially true for diverse learners. If this is the case, one strategy is to have the student sit privately with you and listen to a tape recording or watch a video of the discussion. That way the student can learn to identify the behavior and the difficulties it causes. Because so much goes on in any literature discussion group, the student may be given one or two focus questions for this activity, so that she or he attends to the relevant aspects of the discussion. Without a specific focus, such as "Was someone else talking when I took a turn?" or "What happened when I interrupted the others when they were talking?" the child may pay attention to extraneous factors.

You may need to be explicit about the consequences of the problem because many children (and adults, for that matter) do not spontaneously notice how their actions affect others. For example, you might say, "It is important that you wait until your friends are finished talking to take your turn, because it shows you are listening to them and that you want to hear their ideas. Then they will be ready to listen to your ideas."

ENGAGE THE STUDENT IN SOLVING THE PROBLEM

Next the student and you could brainstorm ways to solve the problem. Providing students the opportunity to think of solutions to the problem will give them an increased sense of control, ownership, and competence, increasing their motivation to participate in the intervention and apply the solution to their discussions. Together you should select one or two promising strategies for the student to use in the next discussion, such as "I will wait until the other student has stopped talking before I take my turn." Role-playing the strategy has been found to be useful so that the child can practice the strategy in a safe environment and the teacher can assess if he or she understands and is able to implement the strategy.

Once you and the student feel the student is ready to put the strategy into use, you might tape record the next discussion and review the recording together. The student should be responsible for determining when the strategy was used or not.

Again, he or she must be able to take responsibility for learning or changing the behavior, with your support. You should discuss when the strategy worked and when it did not and what could be changed for the next time. Individual conferences with the student can continue until the issue seems to improve.

FOCUS ON WHAT THE STUDENT IS DOING RIGHT

Emphasizing what a child does right is important for at least two reasons. First, all of us, but especially students who are struggling, need to know that we are doing something correctly. The intense interactions about problem areas described above can be discouraging if the student thinks that is all the teacher notices about him or her. We all have known adults who only tell us what we do wrong, not what we do right, and we don't like it! If we can, we avoid those folks. So you should find opportunities throughout the day to "catch the student doing well" on a variety of tasks. This strategy builds confidence as well as helps the student to be willing to work on solving a problem.

Second, learners need to know when they are doing something right so they will keep doing it. Sometimes we don't recognize when we are doing something right. Especially when students are first learning to identify and use a strategy, they may not be aware that they are using the strategy correctly. They focus on their failures and don't even notice their own successes. Further, they may be doing part of the strategy correctly, but not the entire strategy. Focusing on what is still wrong provides only part of the picture. An observant teacher will keep an eye on the student and reinforce even partially correct use of the strategy. The "good news/bad news" approach can be useful here: "Sharice, I noticed that during the first part of the discussion you made two comments and you asked Kate to explain a comment she made. Super! Now let's work on making at least four comments overall, so that you are a part of the whole discussion."

Steps in Engaging Students in Problem Solving

- ◆ Make a statement which identifies the problem, the consequences of the problem, and engages the student.

- ◆ Help the student learn to identify the problem.

- ◆ Engage the student in finding strategies to solve the problem.

- ◆ Select a strategy with the student's help.

- ◆ Practice the strategy.

- ◆ Help students monitor their implementation of the strategy.

- ◆ Make sure to focus on what a student is doing right.

Final Thoughts

There has been relatively little research to guide decisions about literature circles and students with diverse needs, but flexibility appears to be an important factor. Literature circles can be tinkered with in many ways to meet your students' needs. It is a challenge, and sometimes you will succeed and at other times you will not. But as a teacher you make a real difference in supporting students simply by being sensitive to their many diverse needs.

Bibliography
of Children's Books

Armstrong, W.H. 1969. *Sounder*. New York: HarperCollins.

Avi. 1991. *Nothing but the Truth: A documentary novel*. New York: Orchard Books.

Avi. 1992. *The True Confessions of Charlotte Doyle*. New York: Avon.

Avi. 1997. *What Do Fish Have to Do With Anything? And Other Stories*. Cambridge, MA: Candlewick Press.

Base, G. 1993. *Animalia*. New York: Scholastic.

Beatty, P. 1987. *Charley Skedaddle*. New York: William Morrow.

Byars, B. 1970. *The Summer of the Swans*. New York: Viking Press.

Byars, B. 1993. *The Pinballs*. New York: HarperCollins.

Byars, B. 1996. *Cracker Jackson*. New York: Penguin Putnam.

Cameron, P. 1961. *I Can't Said the Ant*. New York: Putnam.

Cannon, J. 1993. *Stellaluna*. San Diego: Harcourt Brace.

Cushman, K. 1995. *The Midwife's Apprentice*. New York: HarperCollins.

Dahl, R. 1982. *The BFG*. New York: Farrar, Straus and Giroux.

Durell, A., and Sachs, M. (Eds.) 1990. *The Big Book for Peace*. New York: Dutton Children's Books.

Fitzhugh, L. 1964. *Harriet the Spy*. New York: Harper & Row.

Geisel, T.S. 1971. *The Lorax*. New York: Random House.

George, J.C. 1972. *Julie of the Wolves*. New York: Harper & Row.

George, J.C., Durell, A. (Ed.), and Paterson, K. (Ed.) 1993. *The Big Book for Our Planet*. New York: Dutton Children's Books.

Gipson, F. 1956. *Old Yeller*. New York: Harper & Row.

Henkes, K. 1991. *Chrysanthemum*. New York: Greenwillow Books.

Hoffman, M. 1991. *Amazing Grace*. New York: Dial Books for Young Readers.

Howe, J. 1987. *I Wish I Were a Butterfly*. San Diego: Harcourt Brace.

Hunt, I. 1965. *Across Five Aprils*. New York: Berkeley Books.

Konigsburg, E.L. 1972. *From the Mixed-up Files of Mrs. Basil E. Frankweiler*. New York: Simon & Schuster Children's Publishing.

Konigsburg, E.L. 1989. "Camp Fat," from *Altogether, One at a Time*. New York: Aladdin Books.

Lionni, L. 1997. *Frederick's Fables: A Treasury of 16 Favorite Leo Lionni Stories*. New York: Knopf.

Lowry, L. 1979. *Anastasia Krupnik*. Boston: Houghton Mifflin.

Mochizuki, K. 1993. *Baseball Saved Us*. New York: Lee & Low Books.

Mollel, T. 1992. *A Promise to the Sun: A Story of Africa*. New York: Little Brown.

Munsch, R. 1989. *Love You Forever*. New York: Firefly Books.

Naylor, P.R. 1991. *Shiloh*. New York: Dell.

O'Brien, R.C. 1971. *Mrs. Frisby and the Rats of NIMH*. New York: Aladdin.

O'Dell, S. 1970. *Sing Down the Moon*. Boston: Houghton Mifflin.

Paterson, K. 1988. *Angels and Other Strangers: Family Christmas Stories*. New York: HarperCollins.

Paterson, K. 1992. *The King's Equal*. New York: HarperCollins.

Paulsen, G. 1987. *Hatchet*. New York: Puffin Books.

Ringgold, F. 1991. *Tar Beach*. New York: Crown Publishing Group.

Schlein, M. 1992. *The Year of the Panda*. New York: HarperCollins.

Sendak, M. 1967. *Where the Wild Things Are*. New York: HarperCollins

Shannon, D. 1998. *A Bad Case of Stripes*. New York: Blue Sky Press.

Silverstein, S. 1986. *The Giving Tree*. New York: HarperCollins.

Slote, A. 1992. *The Trading Game*. New York: HarperTrophy.

Smith, D.B. 1973. *A Taste of Blackberries*. New York: HarperCollins.

Spinelli, J. 1990. *Maniac Magee*. New York: Little, Brown.

Stolz, M. 1965. *The Noonday Friends*. New York: HarperCollins.

Taylor, M.D., 1976. *Roll of Thunder, Hear My Cry*. New York: Puffin Books.

Van Allsburg, C. 1990. *Just a Dream*. Boston: Houghton Mifflin.

Van Allsburg, C. 1991. *The Wretched Stone*. Boston: Houghton Mifflin.

Williams, S.A. 1992. *Working Cotton*. San Diego: Harcourt, Brace, Jovanovich.

Yolen, J. 1981. *Sleeping Ugly*. New York: Coward-McCann.

Yorinks, A. 1986. *Hey, Al*. New York: Farrar, Straus and Giroux

Bibliography
of Professional Books and Articles

Allington, R.L. 1983. "The Reading Instruction Provided Readers of Differing Abilities." *Elementary School Journal*, 83, 548-559.

Allington, R.L. 1991. "The Legacy of 'Slow It Down and Make It More Concrete.'" In J. Zutell and S. McCormick (Eds.), *Learner Factors/Teacher Factors in Literacy Research and Instruction* (pp.19-29). Chicago: National Reading Conference.

Allington, R.L. 2001. *What Really Matters for Struggling Readers: Designing Research-Based Interventions*. New York: Longman.

Ash, B. 1990. "Reading Assigned Literature in a Reading Workshop." *English Journal*, 79, 77-79.

Atwell, N. 1987. *In the Middle: Writing, Reading, and Learning With Adolescents*. Portsmouth, NH: Boynton/Cook.

Berliner, D.C. 1981. "Academic Learning Time and Reading Achievement." In J. Guthrie (Ed.), *Comprehension and Teaching: Research Reviews* (pp. 203-225). Newark, DE: International Reading Association.

Cazden, C. 1987. *Classroom Discourse: The Language of Teaching and Learning*. Portsmouth, NH: Heinemann.

Clay, M. M. 1979. *The Early Detection of Reading Difficulties*. Portsmouth, NH: Heinemann.

Clay, M. M. 1985. *The Early Detection of Reading Difficulties*, third edition. Portsmouth, NH: Heinemann.

Daniels, H. 1994. *Literature Circles: Voice and Choice in the Student-Centered Classroom*. York, ME: Stenhouse.

Day, J. 2000. *What Are We Teaching When We Teach Reading Comprehension*. Unpublished manuscript.

Duffy, G. 1993. "Rethinking Strategy Instruction: Four Teachers Development and Their Low Achievers Understanding." *The Elementary School Journal*, 93, 231-245.

Dysthe, O. 1996. "The Multivoiced Classroom: Interactions of Writing and Classroom Discourse." *Written Communication*, *13*, no. 3 (July), 385-425.

Ellenwood, S., and McLaren, N. 1994. "Literature-based Character Education." *Middle School Journal*, 26, 42-47.

Evans, J. 1996. "Creating Spaces for Equity? The Role of Positioning in Peer-Led Literature Discussions." *Language Arts*, 73, 194-202.

Gambrell, L.B., Wilson, R.M., and Gantt, W.N. 1981. "Classroom Observations of Task-Attending Behaviors of Good and Poor Readers." *Journal of Educational Research*, 74, 400-404.

Garcia, E.E. 1990. "Educating Teachers for Language Minority Students." In W.R. Houston, M. Haberman, and J. Sikula (Eds.), *Handbook of Research on Teacher Education* (pp.717-729). New York: Falmer.

Gee, J. 1992. *Social Linguistics and Literacies: Ideology in Discourses.* New York: Falmer.

Gerla, J.P. 1996. "Response-based Instruction: At-Risk Students Engaging in Literature." *Reading and Writing Quarterly: Overcoming Learning Difficulties,* 12, 149-169.

Gilles, C.J. 1990. "Collaborative Literacy Strategies: 'We Don't Need a Circle to Have a Group.'" In K.G. Short and K.M. Pierce (Eds.), *Talking About Books: Creating Literature Communities* (pp. 55-68). Portsmouth, NH: Heinemann.

Gilles, C.J. 1993. "We Make an Idea: Cycles of Meaning in Literature Discussion Groups." In K. Pierce and C. Gilles (Eds.), *Cycles of Meaning* (pp. 199-217). Portsmouth, NH: Heinemann.

Glazer, S.M., and Brown, C.S. 1993. *Portfolios and Beyond: Collaborative Assessment in Reading and Writing.* Norwood, MA: Christopher-Gordon.

Goatley, V.J. 1996. "The Participation of a Student Identified as Learning Disabled in a Regular Education Book Club: The Case of Stark." *Reading and Writing Quarterly: Overcoming Learning Difficulties,* 12, 195-214.

Goatley, V.J., Brock, C.H., and Raphael, T.E. 1995. "Diverse Learners Participating in Regular Education 'Book Clubs.'" *Reading Research Quarterly,* 30, 352-380.

Individuals with Disabilities Education Act (IDEA) of 1997, HR 5, 150 Cong., 1 Sess. (1997).

Johnston, D. 1999. *Write:OutLoud,* volume 3. Wauconda, IL: Don Johnston Inc.

Johnston, P., and Allington, R.L. 1991. "Remediation." In R. Barr, M.L. Kamil, P.B. Mosenthal, and P.D. Pearson (Eds.), *Handbook of Reading Research* (pp. 984-1012). New York: Longman.

Kelly, P.R., Farnan, N., and Richardson, J.J. 1996. "Reader Response: A Way to Help Children with Learning Difficulties Think About Literature." *Reading and Writing Quarterly: Overcoming Learning Difficulties,* 12, 137-148.

Langer, J.A. 1990. *How Writing Shapes Thinking: A Study of Teaching and Learning.* Urbana, IL: National Council of Teachers of English.

Langer, J.A. 1992. "Rethinking Literature Instruction." In J.A. Langer (Ed.), *Literature Instruction: A Focus on Student Response* (pp. 35-53). Washington, DC: National Council of Teachers of English.

Many, J.E. 1996. "When the Literacy Experience Is a Difficult Experience: Implications for Reader Response Theory for Less Proficient Readers." *Reading and Writing Quarterly: Overcoming Learning Difficulties,* 12, 123-135.

Martinez-Roldan, C.M., and Lopez-Robertson, J.M. 1999-2000. "Initiating Literature Circles in a First-Grade Bilingual Classroom." *The Reading Teacher,* 53, 270-281.

McGill-Franzen, A., and Allington, R.L. 1993. "Flunk 'Em or Get Them Classified: The Contamination of Primary Grade Accountability Data." *Educational Research*, 22, 19-22.

Nielsen, D.C. 1993. "The Effects of Four Models of Group Interaction With Storybooks on the Literacy Growth of Low Achieving Kindergarten Children." In D.J. Leu and C.K. Kinzer (Eds.), *Examining Central Issues in Literacy Research, Theory, and Practice* (pp. 279-288). Chicago: National Reading Conference.

Nystrand, M., and Gamoran, A. 1991. "Instructional Discourse, Student Engagement, and Literature Achievement." *Research in the Teaching of English*, 25, 261-290.

Pierce, K.M., and Gilles, C.J. (Eds.) 1993. *Cycles of Meaning: Exploring the Potential of Talk in Learning Communities*. Portsmouth, NH: Heinemann.

Probst, R. 1981. "Response-based Teaching of Literature." *English Journal*, 70, 43-47.

Raphael, T. 1982. "Question-Answering Strategies for Children." *The Reading Teacher*, 36, 186-191.

Raphael, T., Brock, C., and Wallace, S. 1997. "Encouraging Quality Peer Talk With Diverse Students in Mainstream Classrooms: Learning From and With Teachers." In J. Paratore and R. McCormack (Eds.), *Peer Talk in the Classroom: Learning From Research* (pp. 176-206). Newark, DE: International Reading Association.

Rosenblatt, L.M. 1978. *The Reader, the Text, the Poem: The Transactional Theory of the Literary Work*. Carbondale, IL: Southern Illinois University Press.

Schlick Noe, K.L., and Johnson, N.J. 1999. *Getting Started With Literature Circles*. New York: Christopher-Gordon.

Sheppard, L. 1990. "Our Class Knows Frog and Toad." In K.G. Short and K.M. Pierce (Eds.), *Talking About Books: Creating Literate Communities* (pp. 71-81). Portsmouth, NH: Heinemann.

Short, K.G. 1993. "Making Connections Across Literature and Life." In K. Holland, R. Hungerford, and S. Ernst (Eds.), *Journeying: Children Responding to Literature* (pp. 284-301). Portsmouth, NH: Heinemann.

Smith, F. 1998. *The Book of Learning and Forgetting*. New York: Teachers College Press.

Spiegel, D., and Graham, M. 1996. *Sample Prompts for Literature Discussions*. Unpublished manuscript.

Stallings, J. 1980. "Allocated Academic Learning Time Revisited, or Beyond Time on Task." *Educational Researcher*, 9, 11-16.

Throne, M.J. 1992. "A Special Needs Student in a Reading/Writing Workshop." In J.W. Irwin and M.A. Doyle (Eds.), *Reading/Writing Connections: Learning From Research* (pp. 223-244). Newark, DE: International Reading Association.

Wendler D., Samuels, S.J., and Moore, V. 1989. "Comprehension Instruction of Award-Winning Teachers, Teachers With Master's Degrees, and Other Teachers." *Reading Research Quarterly*, 24, 382-401.

Wiseman, D.L., and Many, J.E. 1992. "The Effects of Aesthetic and Efferent Teaching Approaches on Undergraduate Students' Responses to Literature." *Reading Research and Instruction*, 31, 66-83.

Journal Entry Form

NAME _____

PROMPT _____

Before group meeting: Answer prompt and add any other reflections on the chapter.

_____

_____

_____

_____

After group meeting: Have your thoughts or opinions changed any based on what group members said?

_____

_____

_____

_____

How did your literature circle go today?

_____

_____

_____

_____

Observation Checklist

STUDENT NAME _____

Rubric Items	Date/Comments/Observation
Understanding of Literature Discussion Do the students know what types of things to talk about? Is there trouble beginning a discussion or picking a new topic? *("What do we talk about?")*	
Do the students articulate what confuses them? *("I didn't understand why the character chose to return home.")*	
Do the students theorize about confusing sections of the text? *("I wonder if it means that she was sorry for what she had done?")*	
Do the students give evidence from the text for their opinions and evaluations? *("It says right here in the book that she was afraid.")* What type of evidence do they give? Is it based on their own experiences or the text or something else? *("I would never do that if that happened to me.")* Can the students talk about who else might like the book? *("My little sister would like this book better than I did.")*	
Do the students try to understand the book from others' perspectives, such as the author or main character? *("I think the author was making a point about how tough life was back then." "I don't like that the main character joined a gang, but I guess he felt he had to.")*	

Rubric Items	Date/Comments/Observation
Student Interaction Do the students respond to each other's ideas? What are their responses like? Do they agree or disagree with each other's ideas? *("I agree that she was selfish, but I think she had reasons for being a brat. It wasn't her fault.")*	
Are the students willing to disagree? How do they go about disagreeing if they do? *("I don't think that's right. I think she had a good reason for being mean to her sister.")*	
Are the students willing to share tentative ideas, things they haven't thought through completely? *("I've been wondering if that wasn't because things were different then . . . well not different completely, but . . . do you know what I mean?")*	
Do the students ask questions of others? What types of questions do they ask? *("Did you like the book, Ryan? What do you think the character should have done?")*	
How does student participation change in different groups?	
Critical Thinking Are the students willing to reconsider ideas in light of new evidence? What do students do when presented with conflicting evidence? *("That's a good point . . . I forgot that she had made the promise to her friend.")*	
Do the students actively theorize about the world or are they dependent on others to tell them the right answers? *("Well, it might be that . . ." as opposed to "I don't know. What do you think?")*	

Rubric Items	Date/Comments/Observation
Are the students willing or hesitant to disagree with sources of authority? ("I don't care if the books says . . ." as opposed to "Well, the book says so . . . so it must be true.")	
Does the student see others as sources of expertise on which to draw? ("Let's ask Drew. He knows a lot about baseball.")	
When the students give reasons for their opinions, are those reasons internal ("That doesn't fit my experience") or are they external, depending on outside authorites, including their parents, their peers, their friends, the book, or other adults? ("My teacher last year said it means this.")	
Do the students identify complexity in answers or do they just determine ideas as right or wrong? ("I wonder if she was mean because of all the times people let her down," as opposed to "She was mean and that's all that matters.")	
Do the students look for multiple explanations or does one suffice? ("He joined the army for excitement . . . or maybe he felt he had to join the army to help his sister . . . or maybe he wanted to get out of his terrible home situation.")	
Literary Content knowledge What content knowledge do students use? Do they use terms such as character, setting, tone, theme, foreshadowing? Do they talk about terms without having a name for them?	
Do students notice the sound and feel of language? Do they attend to devices such as metaphor and simile and how they help them enjoy a book?	

Individual Reading/Book Log

NAME _____

Title	Author	Date Began	Date Finished

Student Conference Questions

STUDENT NAME _____

1. What do you like and dislike about literature discussions? _____

Would you use them if you were a teacher? _____

How might you do them differently? (Or would you do them differently)? _____

_____

2. What do you think your teacher wants you to learn from literature discussions?

_____

3. What have you learned recently from literature discussions? What would you like to learn next?

_____

_____

4. Are there any books you have especially enjoyed reading and discussing? Why did you like them?

_____

_____

5. Are there any people you especially like having in your group? Why do you like them?

_____

_____

Class Log

	Student Groups	Date
Group 1		
Group 2		
Group 3		
Group 4		
Group 5		

Teacher Daily Log

Group	Date	Observations	Reflections/ Questions	Strategy Lesson
Group 1				
Group 2				
Group 3				
Group 4				
Group 5				
Whole-Class Discussion				

Group Meeting Log

DATE _____

Group members present _____

Group members absent _____

Did everyone read the chapters and prepare a journal entry? _____

Book and chapters read for today _____

Prompt(s) _____

How did your group feel about this prompt?   use it again   don't like it   use it often

Topics discussed _____

_____

_____

Good things that happened today _____

_____

Were there any problems today? _____

_____

How did your group go today? Was this better/worse than other groups in which you have participated?

_____

_____

Self-Assessment Form

NAME _____

1. What do you do well in literature circle discussions? _____

_____

_____

2. What problems do you have? _____

_____

_____

3. How has your participation in literature circles changed over the last _____ weeks?

_____

_____

4. What is one thing you would you like to get better at in literature circles? _____

_____

_____

_____

Index